Emeril Lagasse Large French Door Air Fryer Oven Cookbook

Quick & Tasty Recipes for you to Air-Fry, Bake, Grill, Broil, Roast, Dehydrate, Toast, Slow cook, and More!

Jared Rodgers

CONTENTS

INTRODUCTION

Welcome to a world where taste and creativity collide as age-old culinary techniques are revolutionized by cutting-edge technology. "Emeril Lagasse French Door Large Air Fryer Oven Cookbook" offers more than just a compilation of recipes. It serves as a portal to discover the limitless potential of air frying.

As a chef, I started my journey in the busy kitchens of well-known restaurants, where the sound of sizzling pans and the delightful aroma of spices filled the air every day. Every dish I created was like a story presented on a plate, combining air frying tradition with my unique culinary style. My personal experience with the air fryer oven has been transformative. It has completely revolutionized my cooking routine, providing a healthier option that doesn't sacrifice any flavor.

This cookbook exemplifies the evolution of cooking, showcasing our ability to adapt and innovate. These recipes are crafted to bring joy and spark creativity, from the initial seasoning to the final garnish. Whether you're a home cook or a professional chef, the air fryer oven is a versatile tool that will enhance your culinary creations.

Join me on this delightful journey, where each meal is a joyous exploration of flavors and a testament to the ease of air frying. Let's embark on this delicious adventure together, discovering new tastes and techniques along the way.

The Evolution of Cooking

Cooking has evolved over centuries through experimentation, cultural exchanges, and technological advancements. The transition from ancient techniques to contemporary appliances such as the Emeril Lagasse French Door Air Fryer Oven exemplifies humanity's ongoing pursuit of streamlined processes, delectable taste, and nourishing sustenance. Join me on a journey through the captivating history of cooking.

The Beginnings: Fire and Stone

Cooking has been around since prehistoric times when our ancestors first discovered fire. This groundbreaking finding enabled them to prepare meat in a way that was easier to digest and less likely to cause harm when consumed. The origins of culinary experimentation can be traced back to the early days of cooking on open flames and hot stones. These basic techniques formed the basis for the wide range of cooking methods we now appreciate.

Ancient Civilizations: Advancements and Innovations

As civilizations emerged, so did advancements in cooking techniques and tools. The Egyptians, Greeks, and Romans contributed significantly to culinary arts:

- **Egyptians** utilized clay ovens to bake bread and cook meat.

- **Greeks** introduced spit-roasting and developed intricate recipes combining various herbs and spices.

- **Romans** built complex kitchens equipped with brick ovens, enabling them to prepare elaborate feasts.

These ancient cultures not only refined cooking methods but also established the importance of food in social and religious contexts.

The Middle Ages: Fusion of Flavors

The Middle Ages witnessed a fusion of flavors and techniques as trade routes opened between East and West. Spices, once a luxury, became more accessible, revolutionizing European cuisine. Cooking during this era was characterized by:

- **Feudal Kitchens**: Large hearths and open fires were central to cooking, with cauldrons and spits being common.

- **Spice Trade**: The introduction of exotic spices from Asia transformed bland dishes into flavorful experiences.

- **Medieval Banquets**: Lavish feasts showcased the culinary skills of cooks, who prepared intricate dishes for nobility.

The Renaissance: Culinary Arts Flourish

The Renaissance period marked a significant transformation in the culinary world. With the advent of new-world ingredients like tomatoes, potatoes, and chocolate, European cuisine became richer and more diverse. Innovations included:

- **Refinement of Techniques**: Chefs began to write cookbooks, sharing their knowledge and techniques.

- **Introduction of New Ingredients**: The Columbian Exchange brought many new ingredients to Europe, expanding the culinary repertoire.

- **Rise of Gastronomy**: The appreciation of food as an art form began to take shape, leading to the development of gourmet cuisine.

The Industrial Revolution: Technological Breakthroughs

The Industrial Revolution brought about monumental changes in cooking technology. The invention of kitchen appliances like the stove, oven, and refrigerator revolutionized home cooking:

- **Stoves and Ovens**: Replaced open hearths, providing more control over cooking temperatures.

- **Refrigeration**: Allowed for food preservation, reducing waste, and expanding culinary possibilities.

- **Mass Production**: The ability to produce kitchen tools and appliances on a large scale made them more affordable and accessible.

The Modern Era: Convenience and Health

In the 20th and 21st centuries, culinary innovation was greatly influenced by the growing emphasis on convenience and health. Our fast-paced lives have given rise to convenient appliances and pre-packaged foods, while an increasing awareness of health has sparked a renewed interest in using natural, nourishing ingredients. Notable progress includes:

- **Microwaves**: Introduced quick and convenient cooking.

- **Blenders and Food Processors**: Made food preparation faster and easier.

- **Air Fryers**: Emerged as a revolutionary appliance, offering a healthier alternative to deep-frying by using hot air to achieve crispy textures with minimal oil.

The Future: Smart Kitchens and Sustainability

In the coming years, cooking is set to become even more thrilling as smart technology and sustainability take center stage. Here are some exciting upcoming innovations:

- **Smart Appliances**: Connected devices that can be controlled remotely and programmed to cook meals to perfection.

- **Eco-Friendly Practices**: Emphasis on reducing food waste and utilizing sustainable ingredients.

- **Personalized Nutrition**: Advanced technology to customize diets based on individual health needs and preferences.

Conclusion

The progress of cooking throughout history is a remarkable reflection of human creativity and flexibility. From the earliest use of fire to the incredible innovation of modern kitchen appliances like the Emeril Lagasse French Door Air Fryer Oven, each step forward has brought us closer to achieving culinary excellence. As we keep pushing the boundaries of innovation, the future is filled with countless opportunities to improve our cooking experiences and provide nourishment in increasingly delightful ways.

Benefits of Using an Air Fryer Oven

Air fryer ovens have completely transformed how we cook at home, providing many advantages that perfectly align with today's fast-paced lifestyles. These versatile appliances are quickly becoming a staple in kitchens worldwide, as they combine the convenience of traditional ovens with the innovative technology of air frying. Let's look at the advantages of using an air fryer oven, focusing on the impressive features of the Emeril Lagasse French Door Air Fryer Oven.

Healthier Cooking

Using an air fryer oven has a major advantage: it can cook food with much less oil compared to traditional frying methods. Air fryer ovens achieve a crispy, fried texture by circulating hot air around the food without excessive oil. As a result, the following occurs:

- **Lower Fat Content**: Reducing the amount of oil used in cooking decreases the fat content of your meals, making them healthier.

- **Fewer Calories**: Cutting back on oil also means fewer calories, which can help with weight management and overall health.

- **Reduced Risk of Health Issues**: Lower consumption of unhealthy fats can reduce the risk of heart disease, obesity, and other health conditions.

Versatility in Cooking

The Emeril Lagasse French Door Air Fryer Oven is for more than just frying. Its versatile design allows you to perform various cooking functions, including:

- **Baking**: Prepare delicious baked goods like cakes, cookies, and breads.

- **Roasting**: Achieve perfectly roasted meats and vegetables with a crispy exterior and tender interior.

- **Grilling**: Enjoy grilled dishes with authentic flavor without needing an outdoor grill.

4

- **Dehydrating**: Make dried fruits, vegetables, and jerky for healthy snacks.

Time Efficiency

Air fryer ovens are designed to cook food faster than conventional ovens. The rapid air circulation technology ensures even cooking and reduces cooking times, which is particularly beneficial for busy households. Benefits include:

- **Quick Meal Preparation**: Enjoy faster cooking times for simple and complex recipes.
- **Convenience**: Save time in the kitchen, allowing you to spend more time with family and friends.
- **Energy Efficiency**: Shorter cooking times can save energy, making air fryer ovens an eco-friendly option.

Ease of Use

Modern air fryer ovens, such as the Emeril Lagasse model, come with user-friendly features that make cooking a breeze:

- **Preset Cooking Programs**: Simplify the cooking process with one-touch settings for everyday dishes.
- **Digital Controls**: Easily adjust time and temperature settings for precise cooking.
- **French Door Design**: The unique French door feature allows for easy access and reduces heat loss when checking on your food.

Consistent and Even Cooking

The hot air circulation technology in air fryer ovens ensures that food is cooked evenly on all sides. This eliminates the need to constantly turn or stir food during the cooking process, resulting in:

- **Perfectly Cooked Meals**: Achieve consistent results with every use, whether you're cooking a small snack or a large meal.
- **No Burnt Edges**: Even cooking prevents overcooking and burning, ensuring your dishes are always delicious.

Space-Saving Design

Air fryer ovens combine multiple cooking appliances into one compact unit, making them an excellent choice for kitchens with limited space. They can replace several kitchen gadgets, such as:

- **Toaster Oven**: Use it for toasting and baking without needing a separate appliance.
- **Dehydrator**: Make healthy snacks without the need for an additional dehydrating device.
- **Grill and Roaster**: Eliminate the need for outdoor grills and large roasting pans.

Easy Cleanup

Cleaning up after cooking can be a hassle, but air fryer ovens are designed to minimize this chore:

- **Non-Stick Surfaces**: Many air fryer ovens come with non-stick trays and baskets that are easy to clean.
- **Dishwasher-Safe Parts**: Removable parts are often dishwasher-safe, simplifying the cleaning process.
- **Reduced Grease**: Cooking with less oil means less grease to clean up, keeping your kitchen cleaner.

Enhanced Flavor and Texture

The air fryer oven's ability to circulate hot air evenly results in food that is crispy on the outside and tender on the inside. This enhances the flavor and texture of your dishes, making them more enjoyable. Key points include:

- **Crispy Exteriors**: Achieve a satisfying crunch on foods like fries, chicken wings, and more.

- **Juicy Interiors**: Retain moisture in meats and vegetables, ensuring they are tender and flavorful.

Conclusion

The Emeril Lagasse French Door Air Fryer Oven is a fantastic addition to any kitchen, offering a wide range of benefits. With its focus on healthier cooking and versatility, this appliance enhances your culinary experience and promotes better eating habits. It also offers time efficiency and ease of use, making it a convenient addition to your kitchen. Whether you're an experienced chef or just starting in the kitchen, an air fryer oven can assist you in creating tasty and healthy meals with ease and incredible taste.

Meet Your Emeril Lagasse French Door Air Fryer Oven

Welcome to the thrilling realm of culinary innovation with the Emeril Lagasse French Door Air Fryer Oven. This versatile kitchen appliance, designed by renowned chef Emeril Lagasse, combines the convenience and functionality of a traditional oven with the best of air frying technology. No matter your level of expertise in the kitchen, the Emeril Lagasse French Door Air Fryer Oven will revolutionize the way you cook. Now, let's explore the features and benefits that make this appliance an essential addition to your kitchen.

Key Features and Components

The Emeril Lagasse French Door Air Fryer Oven has cutting-edge features intended to simplify cooking, speed up the process, and enhance your overall experience. These are the main components and what they do:

1. **French Door Design**

   - **Ease of Use**: The unique French door design allows for effortless opening and closing, making it easy to check on your food without losing heat.

   - **Space Saving**: The doors open outward, providing better access to the interior and saving counter space.

2. **Large Capacity**

   - **Spacious Interior**: With a large cooking capacity, you can simultaneously prepare family-sized meals or multiple dishes. Perfect for entertaining or meal prepping.

   - **Multiple Rack Positions**: Adjustable racks allow for versatile cooking options and better airflow, ensuring even cooking results.

3. **12 Preset Cooking Functions**

   - **Versatility**: The oven comes with 12 preset cooking functions, including air fry, bake, broil, roast, toast, dehydrate, and more. These presets simplify cooking and ensure consistent results.

   - **Customization**: Easily customize time and temperature settings for each function to suit your specific recipe needs.

4. **Rapid Air Circulation Technology**

   - **Healthy Cooking**: This technology circulates hot air around the food, cooking it evenly and creating a crispy exterior without excessive oil.

   - **Efficiency**: The rapid air circulation ensures faster cooking times, saving you time in the kitchen.

5. **Digital Touchscreen Control Panel**

   - **User-Friendly Interface**: The intuitive digital touchscreen makes selecting functions, setting cooking times, and adjusting temperatures easy.

   - **Precision**: Digital controls provide precise cooking settings, ensuring your dishes turn out perfectly every time.

6. **Non-Stick Interior and Accessories**

   - **Easy Cleanup**: The non-stick interior and dishwasher-safe accessories make cleaning a breeze.

   - **Included Accessories**: Comes with a variety of useful accessories such as a baking pan, crisper tray, rotisserie spit, and drip tray to expand your cooking possibilities.

Getting Started

To help you get the most out of your Emeril Lagasse French Door Air Fryer Oven, here are a few tips for getting started:

1. **Read the Manual**

- **Familiarize Yourself**: Before using your air fryer oven, take the time to read through the user manual. It contains essential information on safety, setup, and usage.

2. **Initial Setup**

- **Positioning**: Place your air fryer oven on a flat, stable surface with adequate ventilation. Ensure it is away from walls and other appliances to allow proper air circulation.

- **Cleaning**: Wash the removable accessories with warm, soapy water before use. Wipe down the interior and exterior with a damp cloth.

3. **Preheating**

- **Optimal Cooking**: Preheating your air fryer oven can enhance cooking results. Use the preheat function or manually set the temperature and allow the oven to heat up for a few minutes before adding your food.

4. **Using Preset Functions**

- **Convenience**: Take advantage of the preset cooking functions for everyday dishes. These presets are designed to provide optimal cooking times and temperatures for a variety of recipes.

5. **Experimenting with Recipes**

- **Explore**: Feel free to experiment with different recipes and cooking techniques. The versatility of the air fryer oven allows you to prepare a wide range of dishes, from appetizers to desserts.

Tips and Tricks for Best Results

To ensure you get the best results from your Emeril Lagasse French Door Air Fryer Oven, consider the following tips and tricks:

1. **Avoid Overcrowding**

   - **Airflow**: Avoid overcrowding the cooking racks for the best air frying results. Ensure there is enough space around the food for air to circulate evenly.

2. **Shake or Turn Food**

   - **Even Cooking**: For items like fries or chicken wings, shake or turn the food halfway through the cooking time to ensure even browning and crispiness.

3. **Use Cooking Spray**

   - **Prevent Sticking**: Lightly spray the crisper tray or baking pan with cooking spray to prevent food from sticking and to enhance crispiness.

4. **Monitor Cooking Times**

   - **Check Frequently**: Keep an eye on your food, especially when trying a new recipe. Cooking times can vary based on the quantity and type of food.

5. **Adjust for Personal Preferences**

   - **Customize Settings**: Don't hesitate to adjust time and temperature settings based on your personal preferences and the specific requirements of your recipe.

Conclusion

The Emeril Lagasse French Door Air Fryer Oven is a fantastic kitchen appliance that will enhance your cooking experience. Its wide range of features, intuitive design, and health benefits make it a fantastic addition to any kitchen. Embrace the convenience and creativity it provides, and savor the joy of preparing tasty and nutritious meals for you and your loved ones.

Chapter 1: Breakfast & Appetizers

Air Fryer Breakfast Burritos

Time to Prepare: 15 minutes
Cooking Time: 20 minutes
Number of Servings: 4

Ingredients

- 4 large flour tortillas
- 6 large eggs
- 1/4 cup of milk
- Salt and pepper, to taste
- 1 cup of shredded cheddar cheese
- 1 cup of cooked sausage, crumbled
- 1/2 cup of diced bell peppers
- 1/2 cup of diced onions
- 1/4 cup of salsa
- Cooking spray

Instructions List

1. Preheat your Emeril Lagasse French Door Air Fryer Oven to 350°F.
2. In a medium bowl, whisk together eggs, milk, salt, and pepper.
3. Spray a frying pan with cooking spray and heat over medium heat. Add onions and bell peppers, and sauté until softened, about 5 minutes.
4. Add the sausage to the pan and cook until heated through.
5. Pour the egg mixture into the pan and scramble until fully cooked. Remove from heat.
6. Lay out each tortilla and evenly distribute the egg mixture among them.
7. Top each with shredded cheese and a spoonful of salsa.
8. Roll up the burritos by folding in the sides and then rolling from one end to the other.
9. Spray the air fryer basket with cooking spray and place the burritos seam side down in the basket.
10. Air fry at 350°F for 10 minutes or until the tortillas are golden brown and crispy.
11. Serve hot with additional salsa, if desired.

Nutritional Information (per serving)

- Calories: 380
- Protein: 20g
- Total Fats: 18g
- Fiber: 3g
- Carbohydrates: 34g

Maple Bacon Donuts

Time to Prepare: 20 minutes
Cooking Time: 15 minutes
Number of Servings: 6

Ingredients

- 1 can refrigerated biscuit dough (8 biscuits)
- 1/2 cup of maple syrup
- 4 slices bacon, cooked and crumbled
- 1 cup of powdered sugar
- 1-2 tablespoons milk
- Cooking spray

Instructions List

1. Preheat your Emeril Lagasse French Door Air Fryer Oven to 350°F.
2. Separate the biscuit dough and use a small round cutter to cut out the centers to create donut shapes.
3. Spray the air fryer basket with cooking spray and place the donuts in a single layer, leaving space between each.
4. Air fry the donuts at 350°F for 5-7 minutes or until golden brown, flipping halfway through.
5. While the donuts are cooking, mix the powdered sugar, maple syrup, and milk in a bowl to make the glaze.

6. Once the donuts are cooked, dip the tops into the maple glaze and place them on a wire rack.

7. Sprinkle the crumbled bacon over the glazed donuts.

8. Let the glaze set for a few minutes before serving.

Nutritional Information (per serving)

- Calories: 310

- Protein: 5g

- Total Fats: 14g

- Fiber: 1g

- Carbohydrates: 42g

Vegetable Frittata

Time to Prepare: 15 minutes
Cooking Time: 20 minutes
Number of Servings: 4

Ingredients

- 6 large eggs

- 1/4 cup of milk

- Salt and pepper, to taste

- 1 cup of diced bell peppers

- 1/2 cup of diced onions

- 1 cup of chopped spinach

- 1/2 cup of cherry tomatoes, halved

- 1/2 cup of shredded cheddar cheese

- 1 tablespoon olive oil

- Cooking spray

Instructions List

1. Preheat your Emeril Lagasse French Door Air Fryer Oven to 350°F.

2. In a medium bowl, whisk together eggs, milk, salt, and pepper.

3. Heat olive oil in a frying pan over medium heat. Add onions and bell peppers, and sauté until softened, about 5 minutes.

4. Add spinach and cherry tomatoes to the pan, and cook for another 2 minutes.

5. Spray a baking dish that fits in your air fryer with cooking spray and pour the sautéed vegetables into the dish.

6. Pour the egg mixture over the vegetables and top with shredded cheddar cheese.

7. Place the baking dish in the air fryer basket and air fry at 350°F for 15-20 minutes, or until the frittata is set and golden brown on top.

8. Let it cool for a few minutes before slicing and serving.

Nutritional Information (per serving)

- Calories: 210

- Protein: 13g

- Total Fats: 15g

- Fiber: 2g

- Carbohydrates: 6g

Cinnamon Sugar French Toast Sticks

Time to Prepare: 10 minutes
Cooking Time: 10 minutes
Number of Servings: 4

Ingredients

- 4 slices thick bread, cut into sticks

- 2 large eggs

- 1/2 cup of milk

- 1 teaspoon of vanilla extract

- 1 teaspoon of ground cinnamon

- 1/4 cup of granulated sugar

- Cooking spray

- Maple syrup, for serving

Instructions List

1. Preheat your Emeril Lagasse French Door Air Fryer Oven to 350°F.

2. In a bowl, whisk together eggs, milk, and vanilla extract.

3. In a separate bowl, mix granulated sugar and ground cinnamon.

4. Dip each bread stick into the egg mixture, ensuring it's fully coated.

5. Spray the air fryer basket with cooking spray and place the coated bread sticks in a single layer.

6. Air fry at 350°F for 5 minutes, flip the sticks, and cook for an additional 3-5 minutes, or until golden brown.

7. Remove from the air fryer and immediately roll the sticks in the cinnamon sugar mixture.

8. Serve warm with maple syrup.

Nutritional Information (per serving)

- Calories: 220
- Protein: 8g
- Total Fats: 7g
- Fiber: 2g
- Carbohydrates: 32g

Mini Quiches

Time to Prepare: 15 minutes
Cooking Time: 20 minutes
Number of Servings: 12 mini quiches

Ingredients

- 6 large eggs
- 1/2 cup of milk
- Salt and pepper, to taste
- 1/2 cup of shredded cheddar cheese
- 1/2 cup of diced ham or cooked bacon
- 1/4 cup of diced bell peppers
- 1/4 cup of diced onions
- 1/4 cup of chopped spinach
- Cooking spray

Instructions List

1. Preheat your Emeril Lagasse French Door Air Fryer Oven to 350°F.

2. In a medium bowl, whisk together eggs, milk, salt, and pepper.

3. Stir in shredded cheddar cheese, diced ham or bacon, bell peppers, onions, and spinach.

4. Spray a muffin tin that fits in your air fryer with cooking spray and pour the egg mixture evenly into each cup.

5. Place the muffin tin in the air fryer basket and air fry at 350°F for 15-20 minutes, or until the quiches are set and slightly golden on top.

6. Let the mini quiches cool for a few minutes before removing them from the muffin tin and serving.

Nutritional Information (per mini quiche)

- Calories: 70
- Protein: 5g
- Total Fats: 5g
- Fiber: 0.5g
- Carbohydrates: 2g

Stuffed Mushrooms

Time to Prepare: 15 minutes
Cooking Time: 15 minutes
Number of Servings: 4

Ingredients

- 16 large button mushrooms
- 1/2 cup of cream cheese, softened
- 1/4 cup of grated Parmesan cheese
- 1/4 cup of breadcrumbs
- 2 cloves garlic, minced
- 2 tablespoons chopped fresh parsley
- Salt and pepper, to taste
- Cooking spray

Instructions List

1. Preheat your Emeril Lagasse French Door Air Fryer Oven to 350°F.

2. Clean the mushrooms and remove the stems. Finely chop the stems.

3. In a bowl, mix together the cream cheese, Parmesan cheese, breadcrumbs, garlic, chopped mushroom stems, parsley, salt, and pepper until well mixed.

4. Stuff each mushroom cap with the cream cheese mixture.

5. Spray the air fryer basket with cooking spray and place the stuffed mushrooms in a single layer.

6. Air fry at 350°F for 12-15 minutes, or until the mushrooms are tender and the filling is golden brown.

7. Serve warm.

Nutritional Information (per serving)

- Calories: 110
- Protein: 5g
- Total Fats: 8g
- Fiber: 1g
- Carbohydrates: 6g

Crispy Avocado Fries
Time to Prepare: 10 minutes
Cooking Time: 10 minutes
Number of Servings: 4

Ingredients

- 2 large avocados, ripe but firm
- 1/2 cup of all-purpose flour
- 2 large eggs, beaten
- 1 cup of breadcrumbs
- 1/2 teaspoon of garlic powder
- 1/2 teaspoon of paprika
- Salt and pepper, to taste
- Cooking spray

Instructions List

1. Preheat your Emeril Lagasse French Door Air Fryer Oven to 375°F.

2. Slice the avocados in half, remove the pit, and cut each half into 4-6 wedges.

3. Place the flour in one bowl, beaten eggs in a second bowl, and mix breadcrumbs, garlic powder, paprika, salt, and pepper in a third bowl.

4. Dredge each avocado wedge in flour, dip in beaten eggs, and coat with the breadcrumb mixture.

5. Spray the air fryer basket with cooking spray and place the avocado fries in a single layer.

6. Spray the tops of the avocado fries lightly with cooking spray.

7. Air fry at 375°F for 8-10 minutes, or until golden brown and crispy, turning halfway through.

8. Serve immediately with your favorite dipping sauce.

Nutritional Information (per serving)

- Calories: 220
- Protein: 5g
- Total Fats: 15g
- Fiber: 7g
- Carbohydrates: 19g

Buffalo Cauliflower Bites
Time to Prepare: 15 minutes
Cooking Time: 20 minutes
Number of Servings: 4

Ingredients

- 1 head of cauliflower, cut into florets
- 1/2 cup of all-purpose flour
- 1/2 cup of water
- 1 teaspoon of garlic powder
- 1/2 teaspoon of paprika
- Salt and pepper, to taste
- 1/2 cup of buffalo sauce
- Cooking spray

- Ranch or blue cheese dressing, for serving (optional)

Instructions List

1. Preheat your Emeril Lagasse French Door Air Fryer Oven to 375°F.

2. In a bowl, whisk together flour, water, garlic powder, paprika, salt, and pepper to create a batter.

3. Dip each cauliflower floret into the batter, shaking off any excess.

4. Place the battered cauliflower florets in the air fryer basket, making sure they are in a single layer and not touching each other.

5. Spray the tops of the cauliflower florets lightly with cooking spray.

6. Air fry at 375°F for 10 minutes.

7. Remove the basket, flip the cauliflower florets, and air fry for an additional 8-10 minutes or until crispy and golden brown.

8. In a separate bowl, toss the crispy cauliflower florets with buffalo sauce until evenly coated.

9. Return the cauliflower bites to the air fryer basket and air fry for another 2-3 minutes to set the sauce.

10. Serve hot with ranch or blue cheese dressing, if desired.

Nutritional Information (per serving)

- Calories: 150
- Protein: 5g
- Total Fats: 3g
- Fiber: 4g
- Carbohydrates: 27g

Air Fryer Egg Rolls

Time to Prepare: 30 minutes
Cooking Time: 20 minutes
Number of Servings: 8 egg rolls

Ingredients

- 8 egg roll wrappers

- 1 cup of shredded cabbage
- 1 cup of shredded carrots
- 1 cup of bean sprouts
- 1/2 cup of chopped mushrooms
- 1/2 cup of chopped green onions
- 1 tablespoon soy sauce
- 1 tablespoon oyster sauce
- 1 teaspoon of sesame oil
- 1 teaspoon of minced garlic
- 1/2 teaspoon of grated ginger
- Cooking spray

Instructions List

1. In a large skillet, heat sesame oil over medium-high heat. Add garlic and ginger, and sauté for 1 minute.

2. Add cabbage, carrots, bean sprouts, mushrooms, and green onions to the skillet. Cook until vegetables are tender, about 5-7 minutes.

3. Stir in soy sauce and oyster sauce. Remove from heat and let cool slightly.

4. Lay an egg roll wrapper on a clean surface. Spoon about 1/4 cup of the vegetable mixture onto the center of the wrapper.

5. Fold the bottom corner over the filling. Fold the sides toward the center and roll tightly.

6. Seal the edge with water. Repeat with remaining wrappers and filling.

7. Preheat your Emeril Lagasse French Door Air Fryer Oven to 375°F.

8. Spray the egg rolls with cooking spray and place them in the air fryer basket in a single layer.

9. Air fry at 375°F for 10 minutes, flip the egg rolls, and air fry for another 8-10 minutes or until golden and crispy.

10. Serve hot with dipping sauce of your choice.

Nutritional Information (per egg roll)

- Calories: 160

- Protein: 5g

- Total Fats: 4g

- Fiber: 3g

- Carbohydrates: 25g

Spinach and Feta Stuffed Croissants

Time to Prepare: 15 minutes
Cooking Time: 15 minutes
Number of Servings: 4 croissants

Ingredients

- 1 sheet of puff pastry, thawed

- 1 cup of fresh spinach, chopped

- 1/2 cup of crumbled feta cheese

- 1/4 cup of grated Parmesan cheese

- 1 clove garlic, minced

- Salt and pepper, to taste

- 1 egg, beaten (for egg wash)

- Cooking spray

Instructions List

1. Preheat your Emeril Lagasse French Door Air Fryer Oven to 375°F.

2. In a bowl, mix together chopped spinach, feta cheese, Parmesan cheese, minced garlic, salt, and pepper.

3. Roll out the puff pastry sheet and cut it into 4 triangles or squares.

4. Place a spoonful of the spinach and feta mixture onto each piece of puff pastry.

5. Fold the pastry over the filling and press the edges to seal. Crimp with a fork if desired.

6. Brush each stuffed croissant with beaten egg for an egg wash.

7. Spray the air fryer basket with cooking spray and place the stuffed croissants in a single layer.

8. Air fry at 375°F for 12-15 minutes, or until the croissants are golden brown and puffed up.

9. Remove from the air fryer and let cool for a few minutes before serving.

Nutritional Information (per croissant)

- Calories: 280

- Protein: 9g

- Total Fats: 18g

- Fiber: 2g

- Carbohydrates: 22g

Air Fryer Churros with Chocolate Sauce

Time to Prepare: 20 minutes
Cooking Time: 15 minutes
Number of Servings: 4

Ingredients

- 1 cup of water

- 1/2 cup of unsalted butter

- 1 tablespoon granulated sugar

- 1/4 teaspoon of salt

- 1 cup of all-purpose flour

- 2 large eggs

- 1/2 teaspoon of vanilla extract

- Cooking spray

- 1/4 cup of granulated sugar (for coating)

- 1 teaspoon of ground cinnamon

- 1/2 cup of chocolate chips

- 1/4 cup of heavy cream

Instructions List

1. Preheat your Emeril Lagasse French Door Air Fryer Oven to 375°F.

2. In a saucepan, combine water, butter, sugar, and salt. Bring to a boil over medium-high heat.

3. Reduce heat to low and add flour all at once, stirring vigorously until mixture forms a ball and pulls away from the sides of the pan.

4. Remove from heat and let cool for 5 minutes.

5. Add eggs, one at a time, beating well after each addition. Stir in vanilla extract.

6. Transfer the dough to a piping bag fitted with a large star tip.

7. Lightly spray the air fryer basket with cooking spray.

8. Pipe 4-6 inch strips of dough directly into the air fryer basket, leaving space between each churro.

9. Air fry at 375°F for 10-12 minutes, or until churros are golden brown and crispy.

10. While churros are cooking, prepare the chocolate sauce: In a microwave-safe bowl, combine chocolate chips and heavy cream. Microwave in 30-second intervals, stirring until smooth and melted.

11. In a shallow dish, combine granulated sugar and ground cinnamon.

12. Remove churros from the air fryer and immediately roll them in the cinnamon sugar mixture.

13. Serve warm churros with chocolate sauce for dipping.

Nutritional Information (per serving)

- Calories: 480
- Protein: 6g
- Total Fats: 32g
- Fiber: 2g
- Carbohydrates: 45g

Cheesy Jalapeño Poppers

Time to Prepare: 20 minutes
Cooking Time: 10 minutes
Number of Servings: 4

Ingredients

- 8 fresh jalapeño peppers
- 4 ounces cream cheese, softened
- 1 cup of shredded cheddar cheese
- 1/2 teaspoon of garlic powder
- 1/2 teaspoon of onion powder
- Salt and pepper, to taste
- 1/2 cup of breadcrumbs
- Cooking spray

Instructions List

1. Preheat your Emeril Lagasse French Door Air Fryer Oven to 375°F.

2. Cut jalapeño peppers in half lengthwise and remove seeds and membranes.

3. In a bowl, mix together cream cheese, shredded cheddar cheese, garlic powder, onion powder, salt, and pepper until well mixed.

4. Spoon the cheese mixture evenly into each jalapeño half.

5. Place breadcrumbs in a shallow dish.

6. Roll each stuffed jalapeño half in breadcrumbs, pressing gently to coat.

7. Spray the air fryer basket with cooking spray and arrange jalapeño poppers in a single layer.

8. Lightly spray the tops of the jalapeño poppers with cooking spray.

9. Air fry at 375°F for 8-10 minutes, or until jalapeños are tender and cheese is melted and bubbly.

10. Serve hot.

Nutritional Information (per serving)

- Calories: 180
- Protein: 7g
- Total Fats: 12g
- Fiber: 2g
- Carbohydrates: 12g

Sweet Potato Hash Browns

Time to Prepare: 15 minutes
Cooking Time: 20 minutes
Number of Servings: 4

Ingredients

- 2 large sweet potatoes, peeled and grated

- 1 small onion, grated
- 2 tablespoons all-purpose flour
- 1 teaspoon of paprika
- Salt and pepper, to taste
- Cooking spray

Instructions List

1. Preheat your Emeril Lagasse French Door Air Fryer Oven to 375°F.

2. In a large bowl, combine grated sweet potatoes, grated onion, flour, paprika, salt, and pepper.

3. Mix well until all ingredients are evenly incorporated.

4. Spray the air fryer basket with cooking spray.

5. Form small patties with the sweet potato mixture and place them in the air fryer basket in a single layer.

6. Lightly spray the tops of the hash browns with cooking spray.

7. Air fry at 375°F for 10 minutes.

8. Flip the hash browns and air fry for another 8-10 minutes, or until crispy and golden brown.

9. Remove from the air fryer and serve hot.

Nutritional Information (per serving)

- Calories: 120
- Protein: 2g
- Total Fats: 0.5g
- Fiber: 3g
- Carbohydrates: 27g

Air Fried Sausage Patties

Time to Prepare: 5 minutes
Cooking Time: 12 minutes
Number of Servings: 4 patties

Ingredients

- 1 pound ground sausage (pork or turkey)

- Salt and pepper, to taste
- Cooking spray

Instructions List

1. Preheat your Emeril Lagasse French Door Air Fryer Oven to 375°F.

2. Divide the ground sausage into 4 equal portions and shape each portion into a patty.

3. Season both sides of each patty with salt and pepper.

4. Spray the air fryer basket with cooking spray.

5. Place the sausage patties in the air fryer basket in a single layer.

6. Air fry at 375°F for 6 minutes.

7. Flip the patties and air fry for another 6 minutes, or until fully cooked and browned on both sides.

8. Remove from the air fryer and let rest for a few minutes before serving.

Nutritional Information (per serving, 1 patty)

- Calories: 280
- Protein: 15g
- Total Fats: 24g
- Fiber: 0g
- Carbohydrates: 1g

Mozzarella-Stuffed Meatballs

Time to Prepare: 20 minutes
Cooking Time: 15 minutes
Number of Servings: 4

Ingredients

- 1 pound ground beef
- 1/2 cup of breadcrumbs
- 1/4 cup of grated Parmesan cheese
- 1/4 cup of chopped fresh parsley
- 1 teaspoon of garlic powder
- 1 teaspoon of onion powder

- Salt and pepper, to taste
- 4 small mozzarella cheese balls (1-inch diameter), cut into quarters
- Cooking spray

Instructions List

1. Preheat your Emeril Lagasse French Door Air Fryer Oven to 375°F.

2. In a large bowl, combine ground beef, breadcrumbs, Parmesan cheese, parsley, garlic powder, onion powder, salt, and pepper. Mix until well mixed.

3. Divide the meat mixture into 4 equal portions.

4. Take one portion of the meat mixture and flatten it in your hand. Place a quarter of the mozzarella cheese ball in the center.

5. Shape the meat mixture around the cheese to form a meatball, ensuring the cheese is completely enclosed.

6. Repeat with the remaining meat mixture and mozzarella quarters to make 4 meatballs.

7. Spray the air fryer basket with cooking spray.

8. Place the meatballs in the air fryer basket in a single layer.

9. Air fry at 375°F for 15 minutes, or until the meatballs are cooked through and browned on the outside.

10. Remove from the air fryer and let rest for a few minutes before serving.

Nutritional Information (per serving, 1 meatball)

- Calories: 380
- Protein: 28g
- Total Fats: 25g
- Fiber: 1g
- Carbohydrates: 10g

Chapter 2: Poultry

Lemon Herb Roasted Chicken

Time to Prepare: 15 minutes
Cooking Time: 45 minutes
Number of Servings: 4

Ingredients

- 1 whole chicken (about 4 pounds), giblets removed
- 2 tablespoons olive oil
- Zest of 1 lemon
- Juice of 1 lemon
- 2 cloves garlic, minced
- 1 tablespoon chopped fresh thyme
- 1 tablespoon chopped fresh rosemary
- Salt and pepper, to taste
- Cooking spray

Instructions List

1. Preheat your Emeril Lagasse French Door Air Fryer Oven to 375°F.
2. Rinse the chicken inside and out under cold running water. Pat dry with paper towels.
3. In a small bowl, mix together olive oil, lemon zest, lemon juice, minced garlic, thyme, rosemary, salt, and pepper.
4. Rub the herb mixture all over the chicken, including inside the cavity.
5. Tie the chicken legs together with kitchen twine and tuck the wing tips under the body.
6. Place the chicken breast side up in the air fryer basket.
7. Lightly spray the chicken with cooking spray.
8. Air fry at 375°F for 45-50 minutes, or until the internal temperature reaches 165°F when measured in the thickest part of the thigh without touching bone.
9. Remove the chicken from the air fryer and let it rest for 10 minutes before carving.

Nutritional Information (per serving)

- Calories: 450
- Protein: 50g
- Total Fats: 26g
- Fiber: 1g
- Carbohydrates: 2g

Crispy Buttermilk Fried Chicken

Time to Prepare: 30 minutes
Cooking Time: 25 minutes
Number of Servings: 4

Ingredients

- 4 chicken thighs, bone-in and skin-on
- 1 cup of buttermilk
- 1 cup of all-purpose flour
- 1 teaspoon of garlic powder
- 1 teaspoon of onion powder
- 1 teaspoon of paprika
- 1/2 teaspoon of salt
- 1/2 teaspoon of black pepper
- Cooking spray

Instructions List

1. Place chicken thighs in a bowl and pour buttermilk over them. Let marinate for at least 20 minutes.
2. In a shallow dish, combine flour, garlic powder, onion powder, paprika, salt, and pepper.
3. Preheat your Emeril Lagasse French Door Air Fryer Oven to 375°F.
4. Remove chicken thighs from buttermilk, allowing excess to drip off.
5. Dredge each chicken thigh in the seasoned flour mixture, shaking off any excess.
6. Spray the air fryer basket with cooking spray.

7. Place chicken thighs in the air fryer basket in a single layer.

8. Lightly spray the tops of the chicken thighs with cooking spray.

9. Air fry at 375°F for 25 minutes, flipping halfway through, or until chicken is crispy and cooked through with an internal temperature of 165°F.

10. Remove from the air fryer and let rest for a few minutes before serving.

Nutritional Information (per serving, 1 chicken thigh)

- Calories: 350

- Protein: 25g

- Total Fats: 15g

- Fiber: 1g

- Carbohydrates: 25g

Honey Garlic Chicken Wings

Time to Prepare: 10 minutes
Cooking Time: 25 minutes
Number of Servings: 4

Ingredients

- 2 pounds chicken wings, drumettes and flats separated

- 2 tablespoons honey

- 2 tablespoons soy sauce

- 2 cloves garlic, minced

- 1 tablespoon rice vinegar

- 1/2 teaspoon of sesame oil

- 1/2 teaspoon of ginger paste or minced ginger

- Salt and pepper, to taste

- Cooking spray

Instructions List

1. In a bowl, whisk together honey, soy sauce, minced garlic, rice vinegar, sesame oil, ginger, salt, and pepper.

2. Place chicken wings in a large resealable plastic bag or bowl. Pour the marinade over the wings and toss to coat evenly. Marinate for at least 30 minutes in the refrigerator.

3. Preheat your Emeril Lagasse French Door Air Fryer Oven to 400°F.

4. Remove chicken wings from marinade and shake off excess. Reserve the marinade for later use.

5. Spray the air fryer basket with cooking spray.

6. Arrange chicken wings in a single layer in the air fryer basket.

7. Air fry at 400°F for 12 minutes.

8. Flip the wings and air fry for another 12-15 minutes, or until wings are crispy and cooked through with an internal temperature of 165°F.

9. While wings are cooking, pour the reserved marinade into a small saucepan. Bring to a boil over medium heat, then reduce to a simmer and cook for 5-7 minutes, or until thickened into a glaze.

10. Remove wings from the air fryer and toss them in the honey garlic glaze until evenly coated.

11. Serve hot, garnished with sesame seeds and chopped green onions if desired.

Nutritional Information (per serving, about 6 wings)

- Calories: 380

- Protein: 25g

- Total Fats: 22g

- Fiber: 0g

- Carbohydrates: 20g

BBQ Chicken Drumsticks

Time to Prepare: 10 minutes
Cooking Time: 25 minutes
Number of Servings: 4

Ingredients

- 8 chicken drumsticks

- 1/2 cup of BBQ sauce
- 1 tablespoon olive oil
- 1 teaspoon of garlic powder
- 1 teaspoon of onion powder
- Salt and pepper, to taste
- Cooking spray

Instructions List

1. Preheat your Emeril Lagasse French Door Air Fryer Oven to 400°F.

2. In a bowl, combine BBQ sauce, olive oil, garlic powder, onion powder, salt, and pepper.

3. Pat dry the chicken drumsticks with paper towels.

4. Brush each drumstick generously with the BBQ sauce mixture, coating all sides.

5. Spray the air fryer basket with cooking spray.

6. Arrange chicken drumsticks in a single layer in the air fryer basket.

7. Air fry at 400°F for 20-25 minutes, flipping halfway through, or until chicken is cooked through with an internal temperature of 165°F and the outside is crispy.

8. Remove from the air fryer and let rest for a few minutes before serving.

Nutritional Information (per serving, 2 drumsticks)

- Calories: 380
- Protein: 30g
- Total Fats: 18g
- Fiber: 0g
- Carbohydrates: 22g

Chicken Parmesan
Time to Prepare: 15 minutes
Cooking Time: 20 minutes
Number of Servings: 4

Ingredients

- 4 boneless, skinless chicken breasts
- Salt and pepper, to taste
- 1 cup of breadcrumbs
- 1/2 cup of grated Parmesan cheese
- 1 teaspoon of Italian seasoning
- 1/2 cup of all-purpose flour
- 2 large eggs, beaten
- 1 cup of marinara sauce
- 1 cup of shredded mozzarella cheese
- Cooking spray

Instructions List

1. Preheat your Emeril Lagasse French Door Air Fryer Oven to 375°F.

2. Season chicken breasts with salt and pepper.

3. In a shallow dish, combine breadcrumbs, Parmesan cheese, and Italian seasoning.

4. Place flour in another shallow dish, and beaten eggs in a third shallow dish.

5. Dredge each chicken breast in flour, shaking off excess.

6. Dip chicken in beaten eggs, allowing excess to drip off.

7. Coat chicken in breadcrumb mixture, pressing to adhere.

8. Spray the air fryer basket with cooking spray.

9. Arrange chicken breasts in the air fryer basket in a single layer.

10. Lightly spray the tops of the chicken breasts with cooking spray.

11. Air fry at 375°F for 10 minutes.

12. Spoon marinara sauce over chicken breasts and top with shredded mozzarella cheese.

13. Air fry for another 8-10 minutes, or until chicken is cooked through with an internal temperature of 165°F and cheese is melted and bubbly.

14. Remove from the air fryer and let rest for a few minutes before serving.

Nutritional Information (per serving)

- Calories: 450
- Protein: 45g
- Total Fats: 18g
- Fiber: 3g
- Carbohydrates: 25g

Air Fryer Turkey Breast

Time to Prepare: 10 minutes
Cooking Time: 1 hour
Number of Servings: 4

Ingredients

- 2 pounds boneless, skinless turkey breast
- 2 tablespoons olive oil
- 1 tablespoon chopped fresh thyme (or 1 teaspoon of dried thyme)
- 1 tablespoon chopped fresh rosemary (or 1 teaspoon of dried rosemary)
- 1 tablespoon chopped fresh parsley (optional)
- 1 teaspoon of garlic powder
- 1 teaspoon of onion powder
- Salt and pepper, to taste
- Cooking spray

Instructions List

1. Preheat your Emeril Lagasse French Door Air Fryer Oven to 350°F.
2. In a small bowl, combine olive oil, chopped thyme, chopped rosemary, chopped parsley (if using), garlic powder, onion powder, salt, and pepper.
3. Rub the olive oil mixture all over the turkey breast, ensuring it is evenly coated.
4. Spray the air fryer basket with cooking spray.
5. Place the turkey breast in the air fryer basket, making sure it is not touching the heating elements on top.
6. Air fry at 350°F for 30 minutes.

7. After 30 minutes, increase the temperature to 400°F and continue air frying for another 25-30 minutes, or until the internal temperature of the turkey breast reaches 165°F.
8. If the turkey breast starts to brown too quickly, you can tent it loosely with aluminum foil.
9. Remove the turkey breast from the air fryer and let it rest for 10-15 minutes before slicing.
10. Slice and serve warm.

Nutritional Information (per serving)

- Calories: 300
- Protein: 40g
- Total Fats: 14g
- Fiber: 0g
- Carbohydrates: 0g

Cajun Spiced Chicken Thighs

Time to Prepare: 10 minutes
Cooking Time: 25 minutes
Number of Servings: 4

Ingredients

- 8 bone-in, skin-on chicken thighs
- 2 tablespoons olive oil
- 2 teaspoons of paprika
- 1 teaspoon of garlic powder
- 1 teaspoon of onion powder
- 1 teaspoon of dried thyme
- 1 teaspoon of dried oregano
- 1/2 teaspoon of cayenne pepper (adjust to taste)
- Salt and pepper, to taste
- Cooking spray

Instructions List

1. Preheat your Emeril Lagasse French Door Air Fryer Oven to 375°F.

2. In a small bowl, mix together olive oil, paprika, garlic powder, onion powder, dried thyme, dried oregano, cayenne pepper, salt, and pepper.

3. Pat dry the chicken thighs with paper towels.

4. Rub the spice mixture all over the chicken thighs, coating them evenly.

5. Spray the air fryer basket with cooking spray.

6. Place the chicken thighs in the air fryer basket, skin side down.

7. Air fry at 375°F for 12 minutes.

8. Flip the chicken thighs and air fry for another 12-15 minutes, or until the internal temperature reaches 165°F and the skin is crispy.

9. Remove from the air fryer and let rest for a few minutes before serving.

Nutritional Information (per serving, 2 chicken thighs)

- Calories: 450
- Protein: 30g
- Total Fats: 32g
- Fiber: 2g
- Carbohydrates: 2g

Asian Glazed Chicken Legs
Time to Prepare: 10 minutes
Cooking Time: 25 minutes
Number of Servings: 4

Ingredients

- 8 chicken drumsticks
- 1/4 cup of soy sauce
- 2 tablespoons hoisin sauce
- 2 tablespoons honey
- 1 tablespoon rice vinegar
- 1 teaspoon of sesame oil
- 2 cloves garlic, minced
- 1 teaspoon of grated fresh ginger

- Sesame seeds and chopped green onions, for garnish (optional)
- Cooking spray

Instructions List

1. Preheat your Emeril Lagasse French Door Air Fryer Oven to 400°F.

2. In a bowl, whisk together soy sauce, hoisin sauce, honey, rice vinegar, sesame oil, minced garlic, and grated ginger.

3. Pat dry the chicken drumsticks with paper towels.

4. Place the chicken drumsticks in a large resealable plastic bag or bowl. Pour the marinade over the chicken and toss to coat evenly. Marinate for at least 30 minutes in the refrigerator.

5. Spray the air fryer basket with cooking spray.

6. Remove the chicken drumsticks from the marinade, allowing excess to drip off. Reserve the marinade.

7. Arrange the chicken drumsticks in a single layer in the air fryer basket.

8. Air fry at 400°F for 20-25 minutes, flipping halfway through, or until chicken is cooked through with an internal temperature of 165°F and the outside is caramelized.

9. While the chicken is cooking, pour the reserved marinade into a small saucepan. Bring to a boil over medium heat, then reduce heat to low and simmer for 5-7 minutes, or until slightly thickened.

10. Brush the cooked chicken drumsticks with the thickened glaze.

11. Garnish with sesame seeds and chopped green onions, if desired, before serving.

Nutritional Information (per serving, 2 chicken drumsticks)

- Calories: 350
- Protein: 30g
- Total Fats: 12g
- Fiber: 0.5g

- Carbohydrates: 25g

Garlic Butter Chicken Bites

Time to Prepare: 15 minutes
Cooking Time: 15 minutes
Number of Servings: 4

Ingredients

- 1 pound boneless, skinless chicken breasts, cut into bite-sized pieces
- Salt and pepper, to taste
- 1/2 cup of all-purpose flour
- 2 large eggs, beaten
- 1 cup of breadcrumbs
- 1/2 cup of grated Parmesan cheese
- 1 teaspoon of garlic powder
- 1/2 teaspoon of paprika
- 1/2 cup of unsalted butter, melted
- 4 cloves garlic, minced
- 2 tablespoons chopped fresh parsley (optional)
- Cooking spray

Instructions List

1. Preheat your Emeril Lagasse French Door Air Fryer Oven to 400°F.
2. Season chicken pieces with salt and pepper.
3. Place flour in a shallow dish, beaten eggs in another shallow dish, and combine breadcrumbs, Parmesan cheese, garlic powder, and paprika in a third shallow dish.
4. Dredge each chicken piece in flour, shaking off excess.
5. Dip chicken in beaten eggs, allowing excess to drip off.
6. Coat chicken in breadcrumb mixture, pressing to adhere.
7. Spray the air fryer basket with cooking spray.
8. Arrange chicken bites in a single layer in the air fryer basket.
9. Lightly spray the tops of the chicken bites with cooking spray.
10. Air fry at 400°F for 12-15 minutes, flipping halfway through, or until chicken is golden brown and cooked through with an internal temperature of 165°F.
11. In a small bowl, mix melted butter, minced garlic, and chopped parsley.
12. Toss the cooked chicken bites in the garlic butter mixture until evenly coated.
13. Serve hot, garnished with additional parsley if desired.

Nutritional Information (per serving)

- Calories: 450
- Protein: 30g
- Total Fats: 25g
- Fiber: 2g
- Carbohydrates: 30g

Stuffed Chicken Breasts with Spinach and Cheese

Time to Prepare: 20 minutes
Cooking Time: 25 minutes
Number of Servings: 4

Ingredients

- 4 boneless, skinless chicken breasts
- Salt and pepper, to taste
- 1 cup of chopped fresh spinach
- 1/2 cup of shredded mozzarella cheese
- 1/2 cup of grated Parmesan cheese
- 1/4 cup of cream cheese
- 1 teaspoon of garlic powder
- 1 teaspoon of onion powder
- 1/2 teaspoon of paprika
- Cooking spray

Instructions List

1. Preheat your Emeril Lagasse French Door Air Fryer Oven to 375°F.

2. Season chicken breasts with salt and pepper.

3. In a bowl, combine chopped spinach, mozzarella cheese, Parmesan cheese, cream cheese, garlic powder, onion powder, and paprika.

4. Cut a pocket into each chicken breast without cutting all the way through.

5. Stuff each chicken breast with the spinach and cheese mixture, dividing evenly.

6. Spray the air fryer basket with cooking spray.

7. Place stuffed chicken breasts in the air fryer basket.

8. Air fry at 375°F for 20-25 minutes, or until chicken is cooked through with an internal temperature of 165°F and the filling is hot and melted.

9. Optional: For extra browning, you can spray the tops of the stuffed chicken breasts with cooking spray halfway through cooking.

10. Remove from the air fryer and let rest for a few minutes before serving.

Nutritional Information (per serving)

- Calories: 380
- Protein: 40g
- Total Fats: 20g
- Fiber: 1g
- Carbohydrates: 5g

Buffalo Chicken Tenders

Time to Prepare: 15 minutes
Cooking Time: 15 minutes
Number of Servings: 4

Ingredients

- 1 pound chicken tenders
- Salt and pepper, to taste
- 1/2 cup of all-purpose flour
- 2 large eggs, beaten
- 1 cup of breadcrumbs
- 1/2 cup of grated Parmesan cheese
- 1 teaspoon of garlic powder
- 1/2 teaspoon of paprika
- 1/2 cup of buffalo sauce (such as Frank's RedHot)
- 2 tablespoons unsalted butter, melted
- Cooking spray

Instructions List

1. Preheat your Emeril Lagasse French Door Air Fryer Oven to 400°F.

2. Season chicken tenders with salt and pepper.

3. Place flour in a shallow dish, beaten eggs in another shallow dish, and combine breadcrumbs, Parmesan cheese, garlic powder, and paprika in a third shallow dish.

4. Dredge each chicken tender in flour, shaking off excess.

5. Dip chicken tender in beaten eggs, allowing excess to drip off.

6. Coat chicken tender in breadcrumb mixture, pressing to adhere.

7. Spray the air fryer basket with cooking spray.

8. Arrange chicken tenders in a single layer in the air fryer basket.

9. Lightly spray the tops of the chicken tenders with cooking spray.

10. Air fry at 400°F for 12-15 minutes, flipping halfway through, or until chicken is golden brown and cooked through with an internal temperature of 165°F.

11. In a bowl, mix buffalo sauce and melted butter.

12. Toss the cooked chicken tenders in the buffalo sauce mixture until evenly coated.

13. Serve hot, with ranch or blue cheese dressing on the side if desired.

Nutritional Information (per serving)

- Calories: 450
- Protein: 35g

- Total Fats: 18g

- Fiber: 2g

- Carbohydrates: 30g

Chicken Fajitas

Time to Prepare: 15 minutes
Cooking Time: 20 minutes
Number of Servings: 4

Ingredients

- 1 pound boneless, skinless chicken breasts, thinly sliced

- 1 red bell pepper, sliced

- 1 green bell pepper, sliced

- 1 yellow bell pepper, sliced

- 1 onion, thinly sliced

- 2 tablespoons olive oil

- 1 tablespoon chili powder

- 1 teaspoon of ground cumin

- 1 teaspoon of paprika

- 1/2 teaspoon of garlic powder

- Salt and pepper, to taste

- Flour tortillas, for serving

- Optional toppings: shredded cheese, sour cream, guacamole, salsa

Instructions List

1. Preheat your Emeril Lagasse French Door Air Fryer Oven to 400°F.

2. In a large bowl, combine sliced chicken breasts, bell peppers, onion, olive oil, chili powder, cumin, paprika, garlic powder, salt, and pepper. Toss until well coated.

3. Spray the air fryer basket with cooking spray.

4. Spread the chicken and vegetable mixture evenly in the air fryer basket.

5. Air fry at 400°F for 15-20 minutes, shaking the basket halfway through, or until chicken is cooked through and vegetables are tender.

6. While the chicken and vegetables are cooking, warm the flour tortillas according to package instructions.

7. Serve the chicken and vegetable mixture in warm tortillas.

8. Top with optional toppings like shredded cheese, sour cream, guacamole, and salsa, if desired.

Nutritional Information (per serving, without toppings)

- Calories: 350

- Protein: 30g

- Total Fats: 12g

- Fiber: 4g

- Carbohydrates: 28g

Teriyaki Chicken Skewers

Time to Prepare: 20 minutes
Cooking Time: 15 minutes
Number of Servings: 4

Ingredients

- 1 pound boneless, skinless chicken breasts, cut into 1-inch cubes

- 1/2 cup of soy sauce

- 1/4 cup of water

- 2 tablespoons honey

- 2 tablespoons rice vinegar

- 1 tablespoon sesame oil

- 2 cloves garlic, minced

- 1 teaspoon of grated fresh ginger

- 1 tablespoon cornstarch

- 1 tablespoon water

- Optional garnish: sesame seeds, chopped green onions

Instructions List

1. Preheat your Emeril Lagasse French Door Air Fryer Oven to 400°F.

2. In a small saucepan, combine soy sauce, 1/4 cup of water, honey, rice vinegar, sesame oil, minced garlic, and grated ginger. Bring to a simmer over medium heat.

3. In a small bowl, mix cornstarch with 1 tablespoon water until dissolved. Add to the simmering sauce, stirring constantly until the sauce thickens. Remove from heat and let cool slightly.

4. Thread chicken cubes onto skewers.

5. Spray the air fryer basket with cooking spray.

6. Place chicken skewers in the air fryer basket.

7. Air fry at 400°F for 12-15 minutes, turning skewers halfway through, or until chicken is cooked through with an internal temperature of 165°F.

8. Brush the cooked chicken skewers with teriyaki sauce.

9. Optional: Sprinkle with sesame seeds and chopped green onions before serving.

Nutritional Information (per serving)

- Calories: 280
- Protein: 30g
- Total Fats: 8g
- Fiber: 1g
- Carbohydrates: 20g

Herb-Crusted Chicken Cutlets

Time to Prepare: 15 minutes
Cooking Time: 15 minutes
Number of Servings: 4

Ingredients

- 4 boneless, skinless chicken breasts, pounded to 1/2-inch thickness
- Salt and pepper, to taste
- 1/2 cup of panko breadcrumbs
- 1/4 cup of grated Parmesan cheese
- 1 tablespoon chopped fresh parsley
- 1 tablespoon chopped fresh thyme

- 1 teaspoon of garlic powder
- 1/2 teaspoon of paprika
- 2 tablespoons olive oil
- Cooking spray

Instructions List

1. Preheat your Emeril Lagasse French Door Air Fryer Oven to 400°F.

2. Season chicken breasts with salt and pepper.

3. In a shallow dish, combine panko breadcrumbs, Parmesan cheese, chopped parsley, chopped thyme, garlic powder, and paprika.

4. Coat each chicken breast with olive oil.

5. Dredge each chicken breast in the breadcrumb mixture, pressing to adhere.

6. Spray the air fryer basket with cooking spray.

7. Arrange chicken cutlets in a single layer in the air fryer basket.

8. Lightly spray the tops of the chicken cutlets with cooking spray.

9. Air fry at 400°F for 12-15 minutes, flipping halfway through, or until chicken is golden brown and cooked through with an internal temperature of 165°F.

10. Remove from the air fryer and let rest for a few minutes before serving.

Nutritional Information (per serving)

- Calories: 300
- Protein: 35g
- Total Fats: 12g
- Fiber: 1g
- Carbohydrates: 12g

Spicy Sriracha Chicken Nuggets

Time to Prepare: 20 minutes
Cooking Time: 12 minutes
Number of Servings: 4

Ingredients

- 1 pound boneless, skinless chicken breasts, cut into bite-sized pieces

- Salt and pepper, to taste

- 1/2 cup of all-purpose flour

- 2 large eggs, beaten

- 1 cup of panko breadcrumbs

- 1/4 cup of grated Parmesan cheese

- 1 teaspoon of garlic powder

- 1 teaspoon of paprika

- Cooking spray

- For the Sriracha Sauce:

  - 1/4 cup of Sriracha sauce

  - 2 tablespoons honey

  - 1 tablespoon soy sauce

  - 1 tablespoon rice vinegar

  - 1 teaspoon of sesame oil

  - 1 teaspoon of grated fresh ginger

  - 2 cloves garlic, minced

Instructions List

1. Preheat your Emeril Lagasse French Door Air Fryer Oven to 400°F.

2. Season chicken pieces with salt and pepper.

3. Place flour in a shallow dish, beaten eggs in another shallow dish, and combine panko breadcrumbs, Parmesan cheese, garlic powder, and paprika in a third shallow dish.

4. Dredge each chicken piece in flour, shaking off excess.

5. Dip chicken in beaten eggs, allowing excess to drip off.

6. Coat chicken in breadcrumb mixture, pressing to adhere.

7. Spray the air fryer basket with cooking spray.

8. Arrange chicken nuggets in a single layer in the air fryer basket.

9. Lightly spray the tops of the chicken nuggets with cooking spray.

10. Air fry at 400°F for 10-12 minutes, flipping halfway through, or until chicken is golden brown and cooked through with an internal temperature of 165°F.

11. While the chicken is cooking, prepare the Sriracha sauce by combining Sriracha sauce, honey, soy sauce, rice vinegar, sesame oil, minced garlic, and grated ginger in a small saucepan. Bring to a simmer over medium heat and cook for 2-3 minutes, stirring constantly, until slightly thickened.

12. Toss the cooked chicken nuggets in the Sriracha sauce until evenly coated.

13. Serve hot, garnished with chopped green onions or sesame seeds if desired.

Nutritional Information (per serving)

- Calories: 380

- Protein: 30g

- Total Fats: 12g

- Fiber: 1g

- Carbohydrates: 35g

Chapter 3: Beef, Pork, and Lamb

Air Fryer Ribeye Steak

Time to Prepare: 5 minutes
Cooking Time: 10 minutes
Number of Servings: 2

Ingredients

- 2 ribeye steaks, about 1 inch thick
- Salt and pepper, to taste
- 1 tablespoon olive oil
- 1 tablespoon butter
- Optional: Fresh herbs (such as rosemary or thyme), minced garlic

Instructions List

1. Preheat your Emeril Lagasse French Door Air Fryer Oven to 400°F.
2. Pat dry the ribeye steaks with paper towels and season generously with salt and pepper.
3. Drizzle olive oil over the steaks and rub to coat evenly.
4. Place the steaks in the air fryer basket in a single layer, leaving space between them.
5. Air fry at 400°F for 8-10 minutes for medium-rare, flipping halfway through, or until desired doneness is reached (adjust cooking time for thicker steaks or different levels of doneness).
6. Optional: In the last minute of cooking, add butter, fresh herbs, and minced garlic to the top of each steak.
7. Remove steaks from the air fryer and let rest for a few minutes before serving.

Nutritional Information (per serving)

- Calories: 450
- Protein: 40g
- Total Fats: 30g
- Fiber: 0g
- Carbohydrates: 0g

BBQ Pork Ribs

Time to Prepare: 10 minutes
Cooking Time: 40 minutes
Number of Servings: 2-3

Ingredients

- 1 rack of pork ribs
- Salt and pepper, to taste
- 1 cup of BBQ sauce of your choice
- 1 tablespoon olive oil
- Optional: BBQ rub seasoning

Instructions List

1. Preheat your Emeril Lagasse French Door Air Fryer Oven to 360°F.
2. Remove the membrane from the back of the ribs (if not already removed) and trim any excess fat.
3. Season both sides of the ribs with salt, pepper, and optional BBQ rub seasoning.
4. Rub olive oil all over the ribs.
5. Place the ribs in the air fryer basket, bone-side down.
6. Air fry at 360°F for 35-40 minutes, flipping halfway through, or until ribs are tender and cooked through.
7. Brush BBQ sauce over both sides of the ribs.
8. Air fry for an additional 5 minutes at 360°F to caramelize the BBQ sauce.
9. Remove from the air fryer and let rest for a few minutes before serving.

Nutritional Information (per serving)

- Calories: 600
- Protein: 45g
- Total Fats: 40g
- Fiber: 0g
- Carbohydrates: 25g

Garlic Rosemary Lamb Chops

Time to Prepare: 10 minutes
Cooking Time: 12 minutes
Number of Servings: 2

Ingredients

- 4 lamb loin chops
- Salt and pepper, to taste
- 2 tablespoons olive oil
- 4 cloves garlic, minced
- 2 tablespoons fresh rosemary, chopped
- Optional: Lemon wedges for serving

Instructions List

1. Preheat your Emeril Lagasse French Door Air Fryer Oven to 400°F.
2. Season lamb chops generously with salt and pepper.
3. In a small bowl, mix together olive oil, minced garlic, and chopped rosemary.
4. Rub the garlic rosemary mixture all over the lamb chops.
5. Place the lamb chops in the air fryer basket in a single layer.
6. Air fry at 400°F for 10-12 minutes, flipping halfway through, or until lamb chops reach desired doneness (internal temperature of 145°F for medium-rare, 160°F for medium).
7. Remove lamb chops from the air fryer and let rest for a few minutes before serving.
8. Optional: Serve with lemon wedges on the side.

Nutritional Information (per serving)

- Calories: 500
- Protein: 30g
- Total Fats: 40g
- Fiber: 1g
- Carbohydrates: 2g

Air Fried Meatballs

Time to Prepare: 15 minutes
Cooking Time: 15 minutes
Number of Servings: 4

Ingredients

- 1 pound ground beef (or mixture of beef and pork)
- 1/2 cup of breadcrumbs
- 1/4 cup of grated Parmesan cheese
- 1 egg
- 2 cloves garlic, minced
- 1 tablespoon chopped fresh parsley
- 1 teaspoon of dried oregano
- 1/2 teaspoon of salt
- 1/4 teaspoon of black pepper
- Cooking spray

Instructions List

1. Preheat your Emeril Lagasse French Door Air Fryer Oven to 375°F.
2. In a large bowl, combine ground beef, breadcrumbs, Parmesan cheese, egg, minced garlic, parsley, oregano, salt, and pepper. Mix until well mixed.
3. Form mixture into meatballs, about 1 inch in diameter.
4. Spray the air fryer basket with cooking spray.
5. Arrange meatballs in a single layer in the air fryer basket, leaving space between them.
6. Air fry at 375°F for 12-15 minutes, shaking the basket halfway through, or until meatballs are cooked through with an internal temperature of 160°F.
7. Remove meatballs from the air fryer and let rest for a few minutes before serving.

Nutritional Information (per serving)

- Calories: 350
- Protein: 25g
- Total Fats: 20g

- Fiber: 1g

- Carbohydrates: 15g

- Protein: 30g

- Total Fats: 15g

- Fiber: 0g

- Carbohydrates: 30g

Maple Glazed Pork Chops

Time to Prepare: 10 minutes
Cooking Time: 20 minutes
Number of Servings: 2

Ingredients

- 2 bone-in pork chops, about 1 inch thick

- Salt and pepper, to taste

- 1/4 cup of maple syrup

- 2 tablespoons soy sauce

- 1 tablespoon Dijon mustard

- 1 tablespoon olive oil

- 2 cloves garlic, minced

- Optional: Chopped fresh parsley for garnish

Instructions List

1. Preheat your Emeril Lagasse French Door Air Fryer Oven to 375°F.

2. Season pork chops with salt and pepper.

3. In a small bowl, whisk together maple syrup, soy sauce, Dijon mustard, olive oil, and minced garlic.

4. Brush the maple glaze over both sides of the pork chops.

5. Place pork chops in the air fryer basket in a single layer.

6. Air fry at 375°F for 18-20 minutes, flipping halfway through, or until pork chops reach an internal temperature of 145°F (medium rare) to 160°F (medium).

7. Brush with additional glaze during the last few minutes of cooking if desired.

8. Remove from the air fryer and let rest for a few minutes before serving.

9. Optional: Garnish with chopped fresh parsley before serving.

Nutritional Information (per serving)

- Calories: 400

Beef Wellington Bites

Time to Prepare: 30 minutes
Cooking Time: 20 minutes
Number of Servings: 4

Ingredients

- 1 sheet puff pastry, thawed

- 4 beef tenderloin medallions, about 1 inch thick

- Salt and pepper, to taste

- 2 tablespoons Dijon mustard

- 4 slices prosciutto

- 1 cup of mushrooms, finely chopped

- 2 cloves garlic, minced

- 1 tablespoon fresh thyme leaves

- 1 tablespoon olive oil

- 1 tablespoon butter

- 1 egg, beaten (for egg wash)

Instructions List

1. Preheat your Emeril Lagasse French Door Air Fryer Oven to 400°F.

2. Season beef tenderloin medallions with salt and pepper.

3. Heat olive oil and butter in a skillet over medium-high heat. Add minced garlic and sauté until fragrant, about 1 minute.

4. Add finely chopped mushrooms and fresh thyme leaves to the skillet. Cook until mushrooms release their liquid and become tender, about 5-7 minutes. Season with salt and pepper to taste. Remove from heat and let cool slightly.

5. Roll out puff pastry on a lightly floured surface. Cut into 4 equal squares.

6. Spread Dijon mustard on each square of puff pastry.

7. Place a slice of prosciutto on top of each puff pastry square.

8. Spoon mushroom mixture onto each slice of prosciutto.

9. Place seasoned beef tenderloin medallions on top of the mushroom mixture.

10. Fold the puff pastry over the beef tenderloin, sealing the edges. Trim any excess pastry if necessary.

11. Brush the top and sides of each Beef Wellington bite with beaten egg to create a golden crust.

12. Place Beef Wellington bites in the air fryer basket, seam side down.

13. Air fry at 400°F for 18-20 minutes, or until puff pastry is golden brown and beef reaches desired doneness (medium rare to medium).

14. Remove from the air fryer and let rest for a few minutes before serving.

Nutritional Information (per serving)

- Calories: 600

- Protein: 30g

- Total Fats: 40g

- Fiber: 2g

- Carbohydrates: 35g

Honey Mustard Pork Tenderloin
Time to Prepare: 10 minutes
Cooking Time: 25 minutes
Number of Servings: 4

Ingredients

- 1 pork tenderloin, about 1 lb

- Salt and pepper, to taste

- 1/4 cup of honey

- 2 tablespoons Dijon mustard

- 2 tablespoons olive oil

- 2 cloves garlic, minced

- 1 tablespoon fresh rosemary, chopped

- Optional: Fresh rosemary sprigs for garnish

Instructions List

1. Preheat your Emeril Lagasse French Door Air Fryer Oven to 375°F.

2. Season the pork tenderloin with salt and pepper.

3. In a small bowl, whisk together honey, Dijon mustard, olive oil, minced garlic, and chopped rosemary.

4. Brush the honey mustard mixture over the pork tenderloin, coating it evenly.

5. Place the pork tenderloin in the air fryer basket.

6. Air fry at 375°F for 20-25 minutes, turning halfway through, or until the internal temperature reaches 145°F (medium rare) to 160°F (medium).

7. Remove the pork tenderloin from the air fryer and let it rest for 5-10 minutes before slicing.

8. Optional: Garnish with fresh rosemary sprigs before serving.

Nutritional Information (per serving)

- Calories: 300

- Protein: 25g

- Total Fats: 12g

- Fiber: 0g

- Carbohydrates: 20g

Air Fryer Beef Tacos
Time to Prepare: 15 minutes
Cooking Time: 15 minutes
Number of Servings: 4

Ingredients

- 1 pound ground beef

- 1 packet (1 oz) taco seasoning mix

- 1/4 cup of water

- 8 small corn or flour tortillas

- 1 cup of shredded lettuce
- 1 cup of shredded cheddar cheese
- 1/2 cup of diced tomatoes
- Optional toppings: Sour cream, salsa, guacamole, sliced jalapeños

Instructions List

1. Preheat your Emeril Lagasse French Door Air Fryer Oven to 375°F.

2. In a large skillet, cook the ground beef over medium-high heat until browned and cooked through, breaking it up into crumbles as it cooks.

3. Drain any excess fat from the skillet.

4. Add taco seasoning mix and water to the skillet with the cooked ground beef. Stir to combine and simmer for 2-3 minutes until the sauce thickens.

5. While the beef is cooking, place the tortillas in the air fryer basket in a single layer. You may need to work in batches depending on the size of your air fryer.

6. Air fry the tortillas at 375°F for 3-4 minutes until they are warm and slightly crispy.

7. Remove tortillas from the air fryer and assemble tacos with the seasoned ground beef, shredded lettuce, shredded cheese, diced tomatoes, and any optional toppings you desire.

8. Serve immediately.

Nutritional Information (per serving)

- Calories: 400
- Protein: 25g
- Total Fats: 20g
- Fiber: 4g
- Carbohydrates: 30g

Stuffed Pork Loin with Apple and Sage

Time to Prepare: 30 minutes
Cooking Time: 40 minutes
Number of Servings: 4

Ingredients

- 1 pork loin roast, about 2 lbs
- Salt and pepper, to taste
- 1 tablespoon olive oil
- 1 apple, peeled, cored, and diced
- 1/2 onion, finely chopped
- 2 cloves garlic, minced
- 1/4 cup of breadcrumbs
- 2 tablespoons chopped fresh sage
- 1 tablespoon chopped fresh parsley
- 1/2 cup of chicken broth
- Cooking twine

Instructions List

1. Preheat your Emeril Lagasse French Door Air Fryer Oven to 375°F.

2. In a skillet, heat olive oil over medium heat. Add diced apple, chopped onion, and minced garlic. Cook until softened, about 5 minutes.

3. Remove from heat and stir in breadcrumbs, chopped sage, chopped parsley, salt, and pepper.

4. Butterfly the pork loin roast by making a lengthwise cut down the center, without cutting all the way through, so you can open it like a book.

5. Season the inside and outside of the pork loin with salt and pepper.

6. Spread the apple stuffing evenly over the inside of the pork loin.

7. Roll the pork loin tightly and secure with cooking twine at 1-inch intervals.

8. Place the stuffed pork loin in the air fryer basket.

9. Pour chicken broth into the bottom of the air fryer basket.

10. Air fry at 375°F for 35-40 minutes, turning halfway through, or until the internal temperature of the pork reaches 145°F (medium rare) to 160°F (medium).

11. Remove the stuffed pork loin from the air fryer and let it rest for 10 minutes before slicing.

12. Slice the stuffed pork loin into 1-inch thick slices and serve.

Nutritional Information (per serving)

- Calories: 400

- Protein: 40g

- Total Fats: 18g

- Fiber: 2g

- Carbohydrates: 15g

Korean BBQ Beef Short Ribs

Time to Prepare: 20 minutes
Cooking Time: 20 minutes
Number of Servings: 4

Ingredients

- 1 lb beef short ribs, cut into individual ribs

- 1/4 cup of soy sauce

- 2 tablespoons brown sugar

- 2 tablespoons mirin (Japanese rice wine)

- 1 tablespoon sesame oil

- 2 cloves garlic, minced

- 1 tablespoon grated fresh ginger

- 1 green onion, thinly sliced (for garnish)

- Toasted sesame seeds (for garnish)

Instructions List

1. Preheat your Emeril Lagasse French Door Air Fryer Oven to 400°F.

2. In a bowl, whisk together soy sauce, brown sugar, mirin, sesame oil, minced garlic, and grated ginger to make the marinade.

3. Place the beef short ribs in a shallow dish or resealable plastic bag and pour the marinade over them. Ensure the ribs are well coated. Marinate for at least 30 minutes, or up to 2 hours in the refrigerator.

4. Remove the beef short ribs from the marinade and shake off any excess.

5. Place the marinated beef short ribs in the air fryer basket in a single layer.

6. Air fry at 400°F for 18-20 minutes, turning halfway through, or until the ribs are cooked to your desired doneness.

7. Remove the Korean BBQ beef short ribs from the air fryer and garnish with sliced green onions and toasted sesame seeds.

8. Serve immediately.

Nutritional Information (per serving)

- Calories: 350

- Protein: 25g

- Total Fats: 20g

- Fiber: 1g

- Carbohydrates: 15g

Air Fryer Lamb Kofta

Time to Prepare: 20 minutes
Cooking Time: 15 minutes
Number of Servings: 4

Ingredients

- 1 lb ground lamb

- 1 small onion, finely chopped

- 2 cloves garlic, minced

- 2 tablespoons chopped fresh parsley

- 1 tablespoon chopped fresh mint

- 1 teaspoon of ground cumin

- 1 teaspoon of ground coriander

- 1/2 teaspoon of ground cinnamon

- Salt and pepper, to taste

- Olive oil, for brushing

- Yogurt sauce or tzatziki, for serving (optional)

Instructions List

1. Preheat your Emeril Lagasse French Door Air Fryer Oven to 375°F.

2. In a large bowl, combine ground lamb, finely chopped onion, minced garlic, chopped parsley, chopped mint, ground cumin, ground coriander, ground cinnamon, salt, and pepper. Mix until well mixed.

3. Divide the lamb mixture into equal portions and shape each portion into a cylindrical or oval-shaped kofta.

4. Lightly brush the koftas with olive oil.

5. Place the koftas in the air fryer basket in a single layer, leaving space between each kofta.

6. Air fry at 375°F for 12-15 minutes, turning halfway through, or until the koftas are browned and cooked through.

7. Remove the lamb koftas from the air fryer and let them rest for a few minutes before serving.

8. Serve with yogurt sauce or tzatziki on the side, if desired.

Nutritional Information (per serving)

- Calories: 350

- Protein: 25g

- Total Fats: 25g

- Fiber: 1g

- Carbohydrates: 5g

Crispy Pork Schnitzel
Time to Prepare: 15 minutes
Cooking Time: 15 minutes
Number of Servings: 4

Ingredients

- 4 boneless pork chops, about 1/2 inch thick

- Salt and pepper, to taste

- 1/2 cup of all-purpose flour

- 2 large eggs

- 1 cup of breadcrumbs (preferably panko)

- 1/2 cup of grated Parmesan cheese

- 1 teaspoon of paprika

- Cooking spray or olive oil spray

Instructions List

1. Preheat your Emeril Lagasse French Door Air Fryer Oven to 400°F.

2. Season the pork chops with salt and pepper on both sides.

3. Set up a breading station: Place flour in one shallow dish, beaten eggs in another dish, and combine breadcrumbs, grated Parmesan cheese, and paprika in a third dish.

4. Dredge each pork chop in the flour, shaking off any excess.

5. Dip the floured pork chops into the beaten eggs, allowing any excess to drip off.

6. Press each pork chop into the breadcrumb mixture, ensuring they are evenly coated.

7. Lightly spray the breaded pork chops with cooking spray or brush with olive oil spray to help them crisp up.

8. Place the breaded pork chops in the air fryer basket in a single layer, without overcrowding.

9. Air fry at 400°F for 12-15 minutes, turning halfway through, or until the pork chops are golden brown and cooked through.

10. Remove the crispy pork schnitzel from the air fryer and serve immediately.

Nutritional Information (per serving)

- Calories: 400

- Protein: 35g

- Total Fats: 20g

- Fiber: 2g

- Carbohydrates: 20g

Beef and Cheese Empanadas
Time to Prepare: 30 minutes
Cooking Time: 15 minutes
Number of Servings: 6

Ingredients

- 1 lb ground beef

- 1 small onion, finely chopped
- 2 cloves garlic, minced
- 1/2 teaspoon of ground cumin
- 1/2 teaspoon of paprika
- Salt and pepper, to taste
- 1 cup of shredded mozzarella cheese
- 1/4 cup of chopped fresh cilantro
- 1 package (about 12 oz) empanada dough or refrigerated pie crust
- 1 egg, beaten (for egg wash)
- Cooking spray or olive oil spray

Instructions List

1. Preheat your Emeril Lagasse French Door Air Fryer Oven to 375°F.

2. In a skillet, cook ground beef over medium-high heat until browned, breaking it up with a spoon as it cooks.

3. Add chopped onion and minced garlic to the skillet with the beef. Cook until onion is softened, about 3-4 minutes.

4. Stir in ground cumin, paprika, salt, and pepper. Cook for another 1-2 minutes until fragrant.

5. Remove the skillet from heat and let the beef mixture cool slightly.

6. Stir in shredded mozzarella cheese and chopped fresh cilantro into the beef mixture.

7. Roll out the empanada dough or pie crust on a lightly floured surface. Use a round cutter (about 4-5 inches in diameter) to cut out circles from the dough.

8. Place a spoonful of the beef and cheese filling in the center of each dough circle.

9. Fold the dough over the filling to create a half-moon shape. Use a fork to press and seal the edges of the empanadas.

10. Brush the empanadas with beaten egg for a golden finish.

11. Lightly spray the air fryer basket with cooking spray or olive oil spray.

12. Arrange the empanadas in the air fryer basket in a single layer, without overcrowding.

13. Air fry at 375°F for 12-15 minutes, or until the empanadas are golden brown and crispy.

14. Remove the beef and cheese empanadas from the air fryer and let them cool slightly before serving.

Nutritional Information (per serving)

- Calories: 350
- Protein: 20g
- Total Fats: 18g
- Fiber: 2g
- Carbohydrates: 25g

Spicy Italian Sausage Links

Time to Prepare: 5 minutes
Cooking Time: 20 minutes
Number of Servings: 4

Ingredients

- 1 lb spicy Italian sausage links
- Cooking spray or olive oil spray

Instructions List

1. Preheat your Emeril Lagasse French Door Air Fryer Oven to 375°F.

2. Lightly spray the air fryer basket with cooking spray or olive oil spray.

3. Place the spicy Italian sausage links in the air fryer basket in a single layer, without overcrowding.

4. Air fry at 375°F for 18-20 minutes, turning halfway through, or until the sausage links are browned and cooked through.

5. Remove the spicy Italian sausage links from the air fryer and let them rest for a few minutes before serving.

Nutritional Information (per serving)

- Calories: 300
- Protein: 15g

- Total Fats: 25g

- Fiber: 0g

- Carbohydrates: 2g

Teriyaki Glazed Pork Belly

Time to Prepare: 10 minutes
Cooking Time: 25 minutes
Number of Servings: 4

Ingredients

- 1 lb pork belly, sliced into 1/2-inch thick pieces

- 1/4 cup of teriyaki sauce

- 2 tablespoons soy sauce

- 2 tablespoons honey

- 1 tablespoon rice vinegar

- 2 cloves garlic, minced

- 1 teaspoon of grated ginger

- 1 tablespoon sesame seeds (optional)

- Sliced green onions, for garnish (optional)

Instructions List

1. Preheat your Emeril Lagasse French Door Air Fryer Oven to 400°F.

2. In a bowl, whisk together teriyaki sauce, soy sauce, honey, rice vinegar, minced garlic, and grated ginger.

3. Place the pork belly slices in a shallow dish or resealable bag. Pour half of the teriyaki mixture over the pork belly, tossing to coat evenly. Reserve the remaining sauce for later.

4. Arrange the marinated pork belly slices in the air fryer basket in a single layer, without overcrowding.

5. Air fry at 400°F for 20-25 minutes, turning halfway through, or until the pork belly is caramelized and cooked through.

6. During the last 5 minutes of cooking, brush the reserved teriyaki glaze over the pork belly slices.

7. Remove the teriyaki glazed pork belly from the air fryer and sprinkle with sesame seeds and sliced green onions, if desired.

8. Serve hot with rice or your favorite side dishes.

Nutritional Information (per serving)

- Calories: 400

- Protein: 20g

- Total Fats: 30g

- Fiber: 0.5g

- Carbohydrates: 15g

Chapter 4: Pizzas, Sandwiches, and Burgers

Margherita Pizza

Time to Prepare: 15 minutes
Cooking Time: 10 minutes
Number of Servings: 2

Ingredients

- 1 pre-made pizza dough ball (about 8-10 oz)
- 1/2 cup of marinara sauce
- 1 cup of shredded mozzarella cheese
- 1-2 ripe tomatoes, thinly sliced
- Fresh basil leaves, torn or chopped
- Olive oil, for drizzling
- Salt and pepper, to taste

Instructions List

1. Preheat your Emeril Lagasse French Door Large Air Fryer Oven to 400°F.
2. Roll out the pizza dough on a lightly floured surface to your desired thickness.
3. Transfer the rolled-out dough to a piece of parchment paper that will fit in your air fryer basket.
4. Spread marinara sauce evenly over the pizza dough, leaving a small border around the edges.
5. Sprinkle shredded mozzarella cheese over the sauce.
6. Arrange thinly sliced tomatoes on top of the cheese.
7. Season with salt and pepper to taste.
8. Carefully transfer the parchment paper with the pizza to the air fryer basket.
9. Air fry at 400°F for 8-10 minutes, or until the crust is golden brown and the cheese is melted and bubbly.
10. Remove the Margherita pizza from the air fryer using the parchment paper.
11. Drizzle with olive oil and sprinkle with torn or chopped fresh basil leaves.
12. Slice and serve immediately.

Nutritional Information (per serving)

- Calories: 600
- Protein: 25g
- Total Fats: 25g
- Fiber: 3g
- Carbohydrates: 70g

BBQ Chicken Pizza

Time to Prepare: 15 minutes
Cooking Time: 10 minutes
Number of Servings: 2

Ingredients

- 1 pre-made pizza dough ball (about 8-10 oz)
- 1/2 cup of BBQ sauce
- 1 cup of shredded mozzarella cheese
- 1 cup of cooked chicken breast, shredded or diced
- 1/4 red onion, thinly sliced
- Fresh cilantro, chopped (optional)
- Olive oil, for drizzling
- Salt and pepper, to taste

Instructions List

1. Preheat your Emeril Lagasse French Door Large Air Fryer Oven to 400°F.
2. Roll out the pizza dough on a lightly floured surface to your desired thickness.
3. Transfer the rolled-out dough to a piece of parchment paper that fits in your air fryer basket.
4. Spread BBQ sauce evenly over the pizza dough, leaving a small border around the edges.
5. Sprinkle shredded mozzarella cheese over the BBQ sauce.
6. Distribute cooked chicken breast evenly over the cheese.

7. Arrange thinly sliced red onion on top of the chicken.

8. Season with salt and pepper to taste.

9. Carefully transfer the parchment paper with the pizza to the air fryer basket.

10. Air fry at 400°F for 8-10 minutes, or until the crust is golden brown and the cheese is melted and bubbly.

11. Remove the BBQ Chicken Pizza from the air fryer using the parchment paper.

12. Drizzle with olive oil and sprinkle with chopped fresh cilantro, if desired.

13. Slice and serve immediately.

Nutritional Information (per serving)

- Calories: 700
- Protein: 35g
- Total Fats: 30g
- Fiber: 3g
- Carbohydrates: 70g

Air Fryer Grilled Cheese Sandwich

Time to Prepare: 5 minutes
Cooking Time: 10 minutes
Number of Servings: 2

Ingredients

- 4 slices of bread
- Butter or margarine, softened
- 1 cup of shredded cheese (such as cheddar, mozzarella, or American)
- Optional: Sliced tomatoes, cooked bacon, or ham

Instructions List

1. Preheat your Emeril Lagasse French Door Large Air Fryer Oven to 350°F.

2. Butter one side of each slice of bread.

3. Place two slices of bread, butter side down, on a clean surface.

4. Sprinkle shredded cheese evenly over the bread slices.

5. If desired, add sliced tomatoes, cooked bacon, or ham on top of the cheese.

6. Top each sandwich with the remaining slices of bread, butter side up.

7. Carefully transfer the sandwiches to the air fryer basket.

8. Air fry at 350°F for 5 minutes.

9. Carefully flip the sandwiches and air fry for an additional 5 minutes, or until the bread is golden brown and the cheese is melted.

10. Remove the grilled cheese sandwiches from the air fryer and let them cool slightly before serving.

Nutritional Information (per serving)

- Calories: 450
- Protein: 20g
- Total Fats: 25g
- Fiber: 3g
- Carbohydrates: 35g

Philly Cheesesteak Sandwich

Time to Prepare: 10 minutes
Cooking Time: 15 minutes
Number of Servings: 2

Ingredients

- 2 hoagie rolls, split
- 1/2 lb thinly sliced ribeye steak
- 1/2 green bell pepper, thinly sliced
- 1/2 red bell pepper, thinly sliced
- 1/2 onion, thinly sliced
- 1 cup of shredded provolone or cheese whiz
- Salt and pepper, to taste
- Olive oil or cooking spray

Instructions List

1. Preheat your Emeril Lagasse French Door Large Air Fryer Oven to 400°F.

2. Heat a skillet over medium-high heat. Add a little olive oil or cooking spray.

3. Add the thinly sliced ribeye steak to the skillet and cook until browned, breaking it apart as it cooks. Season with salt and pepper. Remove from heat.

4. In the same skillet, add the sliced bell peppers and onions. Cook until softened and slightly caramelized, about 5-7 minutes. Remove from heat.

5. Open the hoagie rolls and evenly distribute the cooked steak, bell peppers, and onions on the bottom halves.

6. Sprinkle shredded provolone cheese or add cheese whiz over the steak and vegetables.

7. Place the assembled sandwiches directly on the air fryer rack or a tray that fits inside the air fryer basket.

8. Air fry at 400°F for 5-7 minutes, or until the cheese is melted and bubbly and the bread is toasted.

9. Remove the Philly Cheesesteak Sandwiches from the air fryer and serve immediately.

Nutritional Information (per serving)

- Calories: 600
- Protein: 35g
- Total Fats: 30g
- Fiber: 4g
- Carbohydrates: 45g

Classic Cheeseburger
Time to Prepare: 10 minutes
Cooking Time: 15 minutes
Number of Servings: 2

Ingredients

- 1/2 lb ground beef
- Salt and pepper, to taste
- 2 slices cheese (cheddar, American, or your choice)
- 2 hamburger buns

- Optional toppings: lettuce, tomato slices, onion slices, pickles

Instructions List

1. Preheat your Emeril Lagasse French Door Large Air Fryer Oven to 375°F.

2. Divide the ground beef into two equal portions and shape them into patties. Season both sides with salt and pepper.

3. Place the burger patties directly on the air fryer rack or a tray that fits inside the air fryer basket.

4. Air fry at 375°F for 7-8 minutes for medium doneness, flipping halfway through.

5. During the last 2 minutes of cooking, place a slice of cheese on each patty to melt.

6. While the patties are cooking, lightly toast the hamburger buns in the air fryer for 1-2 minutes, if desired.

7. Assemble the burgers by placing the cooked patties on the bottom half of each bun. Add optional toppings as desired.

8. Serve the Classic Cheeseburgers immediately.

Nutritional Information (per serving)

- Calories: 550
- Protein: 30g
- Total Fats: 30g
- Fiber: 2g
- Carbohydrates: 35g

Veggie Supreme Pizza
Time to Prepare: 15 minutes
Cooking Time: 12 minutes
Number of Servings: 2

Ingredients

- 1 pre-made pizza dough (store-bought or homemade)
- 1/2 cup of pizza sauce
- 1 cup of shredded mozzarella cheese

- 1/4 cup of sliced bell peppers (red, green, and yellow)

- 1/4 cup of sliced red onion

- 1/4 cup of sliced mushrooms

- 1/4 cup of sliced black olives

- 1/4 cup of sliced cherry tomatoes

- 1/4 teaspoon of dried oregano

- 1/4 teaspoon of dried basil

- Salt and pepper, to taste

- Olive oil or cooking spray

Instructions List

1. Preheat your Emeril Lagasse French Door Large Air Fryer Oven to 375°F.

2. Roll out the pizza dough on a lightly floured surface to fit the air fryer basket or tray. Transfer the rolled-out dough to a piece of parchment paper.

3. Spread the pizza sauce evenly over the dough, leaving a small border around the edges.

4. Sprinkle shredded mozzarella cheese over the sauce.

5. Arrange the sliced bell peppers, red onion, mushrooms, black olives, and cherry tomatoes over the cheese.

6. Season with dried oregano, dried basil, salt, and pepper.

7. Lightly brush the edges of the pizza crust with olive oil or spray with cooking spray to help them crisp up.

8. Carefully transfer the pizza (on the parchment paper) into the air fryer basket or onto the tray in the air fryer.

9. Air fry at 375°F for 10-12 minutes, or until the crust is golden brown and the cheese is melted and bubbly.

10. Remove the Veggie Supreme Pizza from the air fryer, slice, and serve immediately.

Nutritional Information (per serving)

- Calories: 450

- Protein: 18g

- Total Fats: 18g

- Fiber: 4g

- Carbohydrates: 55g

Air Fried Chicken Sandwich

Time to Prepare: 15 minutes
Cooking Time: 20 minutes
Number of Servings: 2

Ingredients

- 2 boneless, skinless chicken breasts

- Salt and pepper, to taste

- 1/2 cup of all-purpose flour

- 1 egg, beaten

- 1/2 cup of breadcrumbs (preferably seasoned)

- Cooking spray or olive oil

- 2 hamburger buns

- Optional toppings: lettuce, tomato slices, pickles

Instructions List

1. Preheat your Emeril Lagasse French Door Large Air Fryer Oven to 375°F.

2. Season the chicken breasts with salt and pepper.

3. Set up a breading station with three shallow bowls: one with flour, one with beaten egg, and one with breadcrumbs.

4. Dredge each chicken breast in the flour, shaking off any excess.

5. Dip the floured chicken breasts into the beaten egg, allowing any excess to drip off.

6. Coat the chicken breasts evenly with breadcrumbs, pressing gently to adhere.

7. Lightly coat the air fryer basket or tray with cooking spray or brush with olive oil.

8. Place the breaded chicken breasts in the air fryer basket or on the tray.

9. Air fry at 375°F for 18-20 minutes, flipping halfway through, until the chicken is golden brown and cooked through (internal temperature should reach 165°F).

10. During the last few minutes of cooking, toast the hamburger buns in the air fryer if desired.

11. Assemble the sandwiches by placing the cooked chicken breasts on the bottom half of each bun. Add optional toppings as desired.

12. Serve the Air Fried Chicken Sandwiches immediately.

Nutritional Information (per serving)

- Calories: 450

- Protein: 35g

- Total Fats: 15g

- Fiber: 3g

- Carbohydrates: 40g

Pepperoni Calzones
Time to Prepare: 20 minutes
Cooking Time: 12 minutes
Number of Servings: 4

Ingredients

- 1 pound pizza dough, homemade or store-bought

- 1 cup of marinara sauce

- 1 cup of shredded mozzarella cheese

- 1/2 cup of sliced pepperoni

- 1/4 cup of grated Parmesan cheese

- 1 tablespoon olive oil

- 1 teaspoon of dried oregano

- 1/2 teaspoon of garlic powder

- Salt and pepper, to taste

Instructions List

1. Preheat your Emeril Lagasse French Door Large Air Fryer Oven to 375°F.

2. Divide the pizza dough into 4 equal portions and roll each portion into a ball.

3. On a lightly floured surface, roll out each dough ball into a circle, about 6-7 inches in diameter.

4. Spread 2 tablespoons of marinara sauce on half of each dough circle, leaving a small border around the edge.

5. Sprinkle shredded mozzarella cheese over the sauce on each dough circle.

6. Arrange pepperoni slices evenly over the cheese.

7. Fold the dough over the filling to form a half-circle and press the edges firmly to seal. You can crimp the edges with a fork to ensure they are sealed.

8. Lightly brush the tops of the calzones with olive oil.

9. In a small bowl, combine dried oregano, garlic powder, salt, and pepper. Sprinkle this mixture evenly over the tops of the calzones.

10. Place the calzones in the air fryer basket or on the tray in a single layer.

11. Air fry at 375°F for about 10-12 minutes, or until the calzones are golden brown and crispy.

12. Remove from the air fryer and sprinkle grated Parmesan cheese over the hot calzones.

13. Serve the Pepperoni Calzones hot with additional marinara sauce for dipping, if desired.

Nutritional Information (per serving)

- Calories: 480

- Protein: 18g

- Total Fats: 22g

- Fiber: 2g

- Carbohydrates: 51g

Meatball Subs
Time to Prepare: 15 minutes
Cooking Time: 12 minutes
Number of Servings: 4

Ingredients

- 1 pound ground beef
- 1/2 cup of breadcrumbs
- 1/4 cup of grated Parmesan cheese
- 1/4 cup of milk
- 1 egg
- 1 teaspoon of dried oregano
- 1/2 teaspoon of garlic powder
- Salt and pepper, to taste
- 4 hoagie rolls
- 1 cup of marinara sauce
- 1 cup of shredded mozzarella cheese
- Fresh basil or parsley, chopped (for garnish)

Instructions List

1. Preheat your Emeril Lagasse French Door Large Air Fryer Oven to 375°F.

2. In a large bowl, combine ground beef, breadcrumbs, Parmesan cheese, milk, egg, dried oregano, garlic powder, salt, and pepper. Mix until well mixed.

3. Shape the meat mixture into meatballs, about 1 to 1.5 inches in diameter.

4. Place the meatballs in the air fryer basket or on the tray in a single layer.

5. Air fry at 375°F for about 10-12 minutes, shaking the basket halfway through cooking, until the meatballs are cooked through and browned.

6. While the meatballs are cooking, split the hoagie rolls and toast them in the air fryer for about 2-3 minutes, until lightly golden.

7. Once the meatballs are done, assemble the subs: Spread marinara sauce on each hoagie roll. Place cooked meatballs on top of the sauce, dividing evenly among the rolls.

8. Sprinkle shredded mozzarella cheese over the meatballs.

9. Return the assembled subs to the air fryer and air fry for an additional 2-3 minutes, until the cheese is melted and bubbly.

10. Remove from the air fryer and garnish with chopped fresh basil or parsley.

11. Serve the Meatball Subs hot.

Nutritional Information (per serving)

- Calories: 600
- Protein: 32g
- Total Fats: 26g
- Fiber: 4g
- Carbohydrates: 58g

Turkey Club Sandwich

Time to Prepare: 10 minutes
Cooking Time: 5 minutes
Number of Servings: 2

Ingredients

- 4 slices bread (whole wheat or your choice)
- 4 slices turkey breast
- 4 slices cooked bacon
- 2 leaves lettuce
- 2 slices tomato
- Mayonnaise, to taste
- Salt and pepper, to taste

Instructions List

1. Preheat your Emeril Lagasse French Door Large Air Fryer Oven to 350°F.

2. Lay out the bread slices. Spread mayonnaise on one side of each slice.

3. On two slices of bread, layer lettuce, turkey breast, bacon, and tomato slices. Season with salt and pepper to taste.

4. Place the remaining bread slices on top to form sandwiches.

5. Place the sandwiches in the air fryer basket or on the tray.

6. Air fry at 350°F for about 3-5 minutes, until the bread is toasted and the sandwich is heated through.

7. Remove from the air fryer and cut each sandwich in half diagonally.

8. Serve the Turkey Club Sandwiches warm.

Nutritional Information (per serving)

- Calories: 450

- Protein: 25g

- Total Fats: 20g

- Fiber: 4g

- Carbohydrates: 40g

Hawaiian Pizza

Time to Prepare: 10 minutes
Cooking Time: 10 minutes
Number of Servings: 4

Ingredients

- 1 pre-made pizza dough (store-bought or homemade)

- 1/2 cup of pizza sauce

- 1 cup of shredded mozzarella cheese

- 1/2 cup of diced pineapple

- 1/4 cup of diced ham

- 1/4 cup of sliced red onions (optional)

- 1/4 cup of sliced bell peppers (optional)

- Fresh basil leaves, for garnish

- Olive oil spray

Instructions List

1. Preheat your Emeril Lagasse French Door Large Air Fryer Oven to 400°F.

2. Roll out the pizza dough on a lightly floured surface to your desired thickness.

3. Place the rolled-out dough on a piece of parchment paper that fits the air fryer basket or tray.

4. Spread pizza sauce evenly over the dough, leaving a small border around the edges.

5. Sprinkle shredded mozzarella cheese over the sauce.

6. Distribute diced pineapple and diced ham (and optional toppings if using) evenly over the cheese.

7. Lightly spray the edges of the pizza crust with olive oil spray.

8. Carefully transfer the parchment paper with the assembled pizza into the air fryer basket or onto the tray.

9. Air fry at 400°F for 8-10 minutes, or until the crust is golden brown and the cheese is melted and bubbly.

10. Remove the Hawaiian Pizza from the air fryer. Let it cool slightly before slicing.

11. Garnish with fresh basil leaves if desired.

Nutritional Information (per serving)

- Calories: 320

- Protein: 15g

- Total Fats: 12g

- Fiber: 2g

- Carbohydrates: 38g

Bacon Avocado Burger

Time to Prepare: 15 minutes
Cooking Time: 15 minutes
Number of Servings: 4

Ingredients

- 1 lb ground beef

- 1/2 teaspoon salt

- 1/2 teaspoon black pepper

- 4 burger buns

- 4 slices cheddar cheese

- 8 slices cooked bacon

- 1 ripe avocado, sliced

- Lettuce leaves

- Tomato slices

- Red onion slices (optional)

- Ketchup and mustard, for serving (optional)

Instructions List

1. Preheat your Emeril Lagasse French Door Large Air Fryer Oven to 375°F.

2. Divide the ground beef into 4 equal portions. Shape each portion into a patty about 1/2 inch thick. Season both sides of each patty with salt and black pepper.

3. Place the burger patties in the air fryer basket or on the tray. Cook at 375°F for about 7-8 minutes per side, or until the internal temperature reaches 160°F and the patties are cooked through.

4. During the last minute of cooking, place a slice of cheddar cheese on each burger patty and allow it to melt.

5. While the patties are cooking, lightly toast the burger buns in the air fryer for about 2-3 minutes until they are warm and slightly crispy.

6. Assemble the burgers: Place lettuce leaves on the bottom half of each toasted bun. Top with a burger patty with melted cheese.

7. Add two slices of cooked bacon on top of each patty, followed by avocado slices, tomato slices, and red onion slices if using.

8. Spread ketchup and mustard on the top half of the toasted buns if desired, then place them on top of the burgers.

9. Serve immediately.

Nutritional Information (per serving)

- Calories: 640

- Protein: 36g

- Total Fats: 42g

- Fiber: 5g

- Carbohydrates: 28g

Pulled Pork Sandwich

Time to Prepare: 15 minutes
Cooking Time: 4 hours
Number of Servings: 6-8

Ingredients

- 3 lbs pork shoulder or pork butt, boneless

- 1 tablespoon olive oil

- Salt and pepper, to taste

- 1 cup of BBQ sauce

- 6-8 burger buns

- Coleslaw, optional, for serving

Instructions List

1. Preheat your Emeril Lagasse French Door Large Air Fryer Oven to 300°F.

2. Rub the pork shoulder with olive oil, salt, and pepper.

3. Place the pork shoulder in the air fryer basket or on the tray. Cook at 300°F for 3.5-4 hours, or until the pork is tender and easily pulls apart with a fork.

4. Remove the pork from the air fryer and let it rest for about 10 minutes.

5. Using two forks, shred the pork into small pieces.

6. In a large bowl, mix the shredded pork with BBQ sauce until well coated.

7. Place the shredded pork back into the air fryer basket or on the tray. Cook at 375°F for another 5-7 minutes, or until the pork is heated through and slightly caramelized.

8. Toast the burger buns in the air fryer for 2-3 minutes until they are warm and slightly crispy.

9. Assemble the sandwiches: Place a generous amount of pulled pork on the bottom half of each toasted bun. Top with coleslaw if desired, then cover with the top half of the bun.

10. Serve immediately.

Nutritional Information (per serving, based on 6 servings)

- Calories: 550

- Protein: 40g

- Total Fats: 22g

- Fiber: 2g

- Carbohydrates: 45g

Spicy Buffalo Chicken Pizza

Time to Prepare: 15 minutes
Cooking Time: 12 minutes
Number of Servings: 4

Ingredients

- 1 lb pizza dough, store-bought or homemade
- 1/2 cup of buffalo sauce
- 1 cup of cooked chicken breast, shredded or diced
- 1/2 cup of red onion, thinly sliced
- 1/2 cup of bell peppers, thinly sliced (any color)
- 1 cup of shredded mozzarella cheese
- 1/4 cup of blue cheese crumbles (optional)
- 1 tablespoon olive oil
- Salt and pepper, to taste
- Fresh cilantro or parsley, chopped (for garnish)

Instructions List

1. Preheat your Emeril Lagasse French Door Large Air Fryer Oven to 400°F.
2. Roll out the pizza dough on a lightly floured surface into a circle or rectangle, depending on your air fryer basket or tray size.
3. Place the rolled-out dough onto the air fryer basket or tray.
4. Brush the dough with olive oil and season lightly with salt and pepper.
5. Spread buffalo sauce evenly over the dough, leaving a small border around the edges.
6. Distribute the cooked chicken breast, red onion slices, and bell peppers evenly over the buffalo sauce.
7. Sprinkle shredded mozzarella cheese over the top, and if desired, add blue cheese crumbles.
8. Place the pizza into the preheated air fryer oven and cook at 400°F for 10-12 minutes, or until the crust is golden brown and the cheese is melted and bubbly.

9. Once done, carefully remove the pizza from the air fryer using tongs or a spatula.
10. Sprinkle chopped cilantro or parsley over the top for garnish.
11. Slice the pizza and serve immediately.

Nutritional Information (per serving, based on 4 servings)

- Calories: 530
- Protein: 28g
- Total Fats: 19g
- Fiber: 2g
- Carbohydrates: 60g

Mediterranean Veggie Wrap

Time to Prepare: 15 minutes
Cooking Time: 5 minutes
Number of Servings: 2

Ingredients

- 2 large tortilla wraps
- 1 cup of hummus
- 1 cup of baby spinach leaves
- 1/2 cup of cucumber, thinly sliced
- 1/2 cup of cherry tomatoes, halved
- 1/4 cup of red onion, thinly sliced
- 1/4 cup of Kalamata olives, pitted and sliced
- 1/4 cup of crumbled feta cheese
- Salt and pepper, to taste
- Olive oil spray (optional)

Instructions List

1. Preheat your Emeril Lagasse French Door Large Air Fryer Oven to 375°F.
2. Lay out the tortilla wraps on a clean surface.
3. Spread 1/2 cup of hummus evenly over each tortilla wrap.
4. Divide the baby spinach leaves evenly between the wraps, spreading them out over the hummus.

5. Layer cucumber slices, cherry tomatoes, red onion slices, Kalamata olives, and crumbled feta cheese on top of the spinach.

6. Season with salt and pepper to taste.

7. Fold the sides of each tortilla towards the center, then roll tightly to create wraps.

8. Lightly spray or brush olive oil on the outside of each wrap to help them crisp up.

9. Place the wraps seam side down in the air fryer basket or on the air fryer tray.

10. Air fry at 375°F for about 5 minutes, or until the wraps are golden brown and crispy.

11. Remove from the air fryer and let them cool slightly before slicing in half.

12. Serve the Mediterranean Veggie Wraps immediately.

Nutritional Information (per serving, based on 2 servings)

- Calories: 420

- Protein: 13g

- Total Fats: 20g

- Fiber: 9g

- Carbohydrates: 50g

Chapter 5: Fish and Seafood

Air Fryer Fish Tacos

Time to Prepare: 20 minutes
Cooking Time: 12 minutes
Number of Servings: 4

Ingredients

- 1 lb white fish fillets (such as cod or tilapia), cut into strips
- 1 tablespoon olive oil
- 1 tablespoon taco seasoning
- Salt and pepper, to taste
- 8 small flour or corn tortillas
- 1 cup of shredded cabbage or coleslaw mix
- 1/2 cup of diced tomatoes
- 1/4 cup of diced red onion
- 1/4 cup of chopped fresh cilantro
- 1 avocado, sliced
- Lime wedges, for serving
- Salsa, sour cream, or hot sauce (optional), for serving

Instructions List

1. Preheat your Emeril Lagasse French Door Large Air Fryer Oven to 400°F.

2. In a bowl, toss the fish strips with olive oil, taco seasoning, salt, and pepper until evenly coated.

3. Place the seasoned fish strips in a single layer in the air fryer basket or on the air fryer tray.

4. Air fry at 400°F for 10-12 minutes, flipping halfway through, until the fish is cooked through and crispy.

5. While the fish cooks, warm the tortillas according to package instructions or preference.

6. Assemble the tacos: divide the shredded cabbage, diced tomatoes, red onion, and chopped cilantro among the warmed tortillas.

7. Top each taco with a few slices of avocado and a squeeze of lime juice.

8. Place the cooked fish strips on top of each taco.

9. Serve the Air Fryer Fish Tacos with salsa, sour cream, or hot sauce if desired.

Nutritional Information (per serving, based on 4 servings)

- Calories: 340
- Protein: 25g
- Total Fats: 13g
- Fiber: 6g
- Carbohydrates: 32g

Lemon Herb Salmon

Time to Prepare: 10 minutes
Cooking Time: 12 minutes
Number of Servings: 4

Ingredients

- 4 salmon fillets, about 6 oz each
- 2 tablespoons olive oil
- Zest of 1 lemon
- Juice of 1 lemon
- 2 cloves garlic, minced
- 1 teaspoon of dried thyme (or 1 tablespoon fresh thyme)
- 1 teaspoon of dried rosemary (or 1 tablespoon fresh rosemary)
- Salt and pepper, to taste
- Lemon wedges, for serving
- Fresh parsley, chopped, for garnish (optional)

Instructions List

1. Preheat your Emeril Lagasse French Door Large Air Fryer Oven to 400°F.

2. In a small bowl, combine olive oil, lemon zest, lemon juice, minced garlic, dried thyme, dried rosemary, salt, and pepper.

3. Place the salmon fillets on a plate or in a shallow dish. Pour the lemon herb marinade over the salmon, making sure each fillet is well coated. Allow to marinate for 10 minutes.

4. Place the marinated salmon fillets in the air fryer basket or on the air fryer tray in a single layer.

5. Air fry at 400°F for 10-12 minutes, depending on the thickness of the salmon fillets, until the salmon is cooked through and flakes easily with a fork.

6. Remove the salmon from the air fryer and let it rest for a few minutes.

7. Serve the Lemon Herb Salmon hot, garnished with fresh parsley if desired, and lemon wedges on the side.

Nutritional Information (per serving, based on 4 servings)

- Calories: 330
- Protein: 34g
- Total Fats: 20g
- Fiber: 1g
- Carbohydrates: 2g

Coconut Shrimp
Time to Prepare: 20 minutes
Cooking Time: 10 minutes
Number of Servings: 4

Ingredients

- 1 pound large shrimp, peeled and deveined
- 1 cup of shredded coconut (sweetened or unsweetened)
- 1/2 cup of panko breadcrumbs
- 1/2 teaspoon of garlic powder
- 1/2 teaspoon of paprika
- 1/2 teaspoon of salt
- 1/4 teaspoon of black pepper
- 2 eggs, beaten
- Cooking spray or oil for misting

Instructions List

1. Preheat your Emeril Lagasse French Door Large Air Fryer Oven to 375°F.

2. In a shallow bowl, combine shredded coconut, panko breadcrumbs, garlic powder, paprika, salt, and black pepper.

3. Dip each shrimp into the beaten eggs, then coat with the coconut breadcrumb mixture, pressing gently to adhere.

4. Place the coated shrimp on the air fryer tray or in the air fryer basket, leaving space between each shrimp.

5. Lightly mist the coated shrimp with cooking spray or brush with a little oil.

6. Air fry at 375°F for 8-10 minutes, flipping halfway through, until the shrimp are cooked through and the coconut coating is golden brown and crispy.

7. Serve the Coconut Shrimp hot with your favorite dipping sauce.

Nutritional Information (per serving, based on 4 servings)

- Calories: 330
- Protein: 23g
- Total Fats: 20g
- Fiber: 2g
- Carbohydrates: 18g

Garlic Butter Lobster Tails
Time to Prepare: 15 minutes
Cooking Time: 10 minutes
Number of Servings: 2

Ingredients

- 2 lobster tails, thawed if frozen
- 4 tablespoons unsalted butter, melted
- 4 cloves garlic, minced
- 1 tablespoon fresh parsley, chopped

- Salt and pepper, to taste
- Lemon wedges, for serving

Instructions List

1. Preheat your Emeril Lagasse French Door Large Air Fryer Oven to 400°F.

2. Use kitchen shears to cut through the top shell of the lobster tails and then use a knife to cut through the meat.

3. Gently pull the lobster meat slightly out of the shell and place it on top of the shell.

4. In a small bowl, combine melted butter, minced garlic, chopped parsley, salt, and pepper.

5. Brush the garlic butter mixture generously over the exposed lobster meat.

6. Place the lobster tails onto the air fryer tray or in the air fryer basket, ensuring they are not overlapping.

7. Air fry at 400°F for about 8-10 minutes or until the lobster meat is opaque and cooked through, and the shells are bright red.

8. Serve the Garlic Butter Lobster Tails immediately with lemon wedges for squeezing over the top.

Nutritional Information (per serving, based on 2 servings)

- Calories: 240
- Protein: 20g
- Total Fats: 16g
- Fiber: 0g
- Carbohydrates: 2g

Crispy Fish and Chips

Time to Prepare: 15 minutes
Cooking Time: 20 minutes
Number of Servings: 4

Ingredients

- 4 white fish fillets (such as cod or haddock), about 6 oz each
- 1 cup of all-purpose flour

- 1 teaspoon of salt
- 1/2 teaspoon of black pepper
- 1 teaspoon of paprika
- 2 large eggs
- 1 cup of panko breadcrumbs
- Cooking spray or olive oil spray
- 4 large potatoes, peeled and cut into fries
- Salt, to taste
- Lemon wedges, for serving
- Tartar sauce, for serving (optional)

Instructions List

1. Preheat your Emeril Lagasse French Door Large Air Fryer Oven to 400°F.

2. Pat dry the fish fillets with paper towels to remove excess moisture.

3. In a shallow bowl, whisk together the flour, salt, pepper, and paprika.

4. In another shallow bowl, beat the eggs.

5. Place the panko breadcrumbs in a third shallow bowl.

6. Dredge each fish fillet in the seasoned flour mixture, shaking off any excess.

7. Dip the floured fish fillets into the beaten eggs, allowing any excess to drip off.

8. Press the fillets into the panko breadcrumbs, coating both sides evenly.

9. Place the coated fish fillets in the air fryer basket or on the air fryer tray in a single layer. Spray lightly with cooking spray or olive oil spray.

10. Place the potato fries in a single layer in the air fryer basket or on the air fryer tray.

11. Air fry the fish and chips at 400°F for 18-20 minutes, flipping the fish halfway through, until the fish is golden and crispy and the fries are tender and golden brown.

12. Remove the fish and chips from the air fryer. Season the fries with salt to taste.

13. Serve the Crispy Fish and Chips hot with lemon wedges and tartar sauce on the side, if desired.

Nutritional Information (per serving, based on 4 servings)

- Calories: 480
- Protein: 30g
- Total Fats: 12g
- Fiber: 4g
- Carbohydrates: 62g

Honey Soy Glazed Cod

Time to Prepare: 10 minutes
Cooking Time: 12 minutes
Number of Servings: 4

Ingredients

- 4 cod fillets, about 6 oz each
- 1/4 cup of honey
- 1/4 cup of soy sauce (reduced sodium preferred)
- 2 tablespoons rice vinegar
- 2 cloves garlic, minced
- 1 tablespoon fresh ginger, grated
- 1/2 teaspoon of sesame oil
- Sesame seeds, for garnish (optional)
- Green onions, chopped, for garnish (optional)

Instructions List

1. Preheat your Emeril Lagasse French Door Large Air Fryer Oven to 400°F.

2. In a small bowl, whisk together honey, soy sauce, rice vinegar, garlic, ginger, and sesame oil to make the glaze.

3. Pat dry the cod fillets with paper towels.

4. Place the cod fillets in a single layer on the air fryer basket or tray.

5. Brush the cod fillets generously with the honey soy glaze, reserving some glaze for later.

6. Air fry the cod fillets at 400°F for 10-12 minutes, depending on the thickness of the fillets, until the fish flakes easily with a fork and is opaque throughout.

7. Brush the cooked cod fillets with the remaining honey soy glaze.

8. Garnish with sesame seeds and chopped green onions, if desired.

9. Serve the Honey Soy Glazed Cod hot, accompanied by steamed rice and vegetables.

Nutritional Information (per serving, based on 4 servings)

- Calories: 290
- Protein: 28g
- Total Fats: 4g
- Fiber: 0g
- Carbohydrates: 36g

Cajun Catfish

Time to Prepare: 10 minutes
Cooking Time: 12 minutes
Number of Servings: 4

Ingredients

- 4 catfish fillets, about 6 oz each
- 2 tablespoons olive oil
- 1 tablespoon paprika
- 1 teaspoon of garlic powder
- 1 teaspoon of onion powder
- 1 teaspoon of dried thyme
- 1 teaspoon of dried oregano
- 1/2 teaspoon of cayenne pepper (adjust to taste)
- 1/2 teaspoon of salt
- 1/4 teaspoon of black pepper
- Lemon wedges, for serving
- Fresh parsley, chopped, for garnish (optional)

Instructions List

1. Preheat your Emeril Lagasse French Door Large Air Fryer Oven to 400°F.

2. In a small bowl, combine olive oil, paprika, garlic powder, onion powder, dried thyme, dried oregano, cayenne pepper, salt, and black pepper to make the Cajun seasoning.

3. Pat dry the catfish fillets with paper towels.

4. Rub the Cajun seasoning mixture evenly over both sides of the catfish fillets.

5. Place the catfish fillets in a single layer on the air fryer basket or tray.

6. Air fry the catfish fillets at 400°F for 10-12 minutes, depending on the thickness of the fillets, until the fish flakes easily with a fork and is opaque throughout.

7. Remove the catfish fillets from the air fryer and let them rest for a few minutes.

8. Serve the Cajun Catfish hot, garnished with lemon wedges and chopped parsley if desired.

Nutritional Information (per serving, based on 4 servings)

- Calories: 260

- Protein: 30g

- Total Fats: 13g

- Fiber: 2g

- Carbohydrates: 4g

Parmesan Crusted Tilapia

Time to Prepare: 10 minutes
Cooking Time: 10 minutes
Number of Servings: 4

Ingredients

- 4 tilapia fillets, about 6 oz each

- 1/2 cup of grated Parmesan cheese

- 1/4 cup of panko breadcrumbs

- 1 teaspoon of garlic powder

- 1 teaspoon of dried parsley

- 1/2 teaspoon of salt

- 1/4 teaspoon of black pepper

- 2 tablespoons olive oil

- Lemon wedges, for serving

- Fresh parsley, chopped, for garnish (optional)

Instructions List

1. Preheat your Emeril Lagasse French Door Large Air Fryer Oven to 400°F.

2. In a shallow dish, combine grated Parmesan cheese, panko breadcrumbs, garlic powder, dried parsley, salt, and black pepper.

3. Pat dry the tilapia fillets with paper towels.

4. Brush both sides of each tilapia fillet with olive oil.

5. Dredge each fillet in the Parmesan breadcrumb mixture, pressing gently to coat evenly.

6. Place the coated tilapia fillets in a single layer on the air fryer basket or tray.

7. Air fry the tilapia fillets at 400°F for 8-10 minutes, depending on the thickness of the fillets, until the fish flakes easily with a fork and is golden brown and crispy.

8. Remove the tilapia fillets from the air fryer and let them rest for a few minutes.

9. Serve the Parmesan Crusted Tilapia hot, garnished with lemon wedges and chopped parsley if desired.

Nutritional Information (per serving, based on 4 servings)

- Calories: 290

- Protein: 33g

- Total Fats: 14g

- Fiber: 1g

- Carbohydrates: 7g

Air Fried Scallops

Time to Prepare: 10 minutes
Cooking Time: 10 minutes
Number of Servings: 4

Ingredients

- 1 lb fresh scallops, patted dry
- 1/2 cup of panko breadcrumbs
- 1/4 cup of grated Parmesan cheese
- 1 teaspoon of garlic powder
- 1 teaspoon of paprika
- 1/2 teaspoon of salt
- 1/4 teaspoon of black pepper
- 2 tablespoons olive oil
- Lemon wedges, for serving
- Fresh parsley, chopped, for garnish (optional)

Instructions List

1. Preheat your Emeril Lagasse French Door Large Air Fryer Oven to 400°F.

2. In a shallow dish, combine panko breadcrumbs, grated Parmesan cheese, garlic powder, paprika, salt, and black pepper.

3. Pat dry the scallops with paper towels.

4. Brush both sides of each scallop with olive oil.

5. Dredge each scallop in the breadcrumb mixture, pressing gently to coat evenly.

6. Place the coated scallops in a single layer on the air fryer basket or tray.

7. Air fry the scallops at 400°F for 8-10 minutes, depending on the size of the scallops, until they are golden brown and cooked through.

8. Remove the scallops from the air fryer and let them rest for a few minutes.

9. Serve the Air Fried Scallops hot, garnished with lemon wedges and chopped parsley if desired.

Nutritional Information (per serving, based on 4 servings)

- Calories: 250
- Protein: 24g
- Total Fats: 12g
- Fiber: 1g
- Carbohydrates: 12g

Shrimp Scampi

Time to Prepare: 15 minutes
Cooking Time: 10 minutes
Number of Servings: 4

Ingredients

- 1 lb large shrimp, peeled and deveined
- 4 tablespoons unsalted butter, divided
- 4 cloves garlic, minced
- 1/4 cup of dry white wine
- 2 tablespoons lemon juice
- 1/4 teaspoon of red pepper flakes (optional)
- Salt and pepper, to taste
- 2 tablespoons chopped fresh parsley
- Lemon wedges, for serving
- Cooked pasta or crusty bread, for serving (optional)

Instructions List

1. Preheat your Emeril Lagasse French Door Large Air Fryer Oven to 400°F.

2. In a large bowl, toss the shrimp with 2 tablespoons of melted butter, minced garlic, salt, and pepper.

3. Place the seasoned shrimp in the air fryer basket or on the air fryer tray in a single layer.

4. Air fry the shrimp at 400°F for 5-6 minutes, shaking the basket halfway through cooking, until the shrimp are pink and opaque.

5. While the shrimp are cooking, melt the remaining 2 tablespoons of butter in a small skillet over medium heat.

6. Add the white wine, lemon juice, and red pepper flakes (if using) to the skillet. Cook for 2-3 minutes, stirring occasionally, until slightly reduced.

7. Remove the skillet from heat and stir in the chopped parsley.

8. Transfer the cooked shrimp to a serving dish. Pour the buttery wine sauce over the shrimp and toss gently to coat.

9. Serve the Shrimp Scampi hot, garnished with lemon wedges. Serve with pasta or crusty bread if desired.

Nutritional Information (per serving, based on 4 servings)

- Calories: 240
- Protein: 24g
- Total Fats: 12g
- Fiber: 0g
- Carbohydrates: 3g

Teriyaki Salmon Bites

Time to Prepare: 15 minutes
Cooking Time: 10 minutes
Number of Servings: 4

Ingredients

- 1 lb salmon fillet, skin removed, cut into bite-sized pieces
- 1/4 cup of soy sauce
- 2 tablespoons honey
- 2 tablespoons rice vinegar
- 1 tablespoon mirin (Japanese sweet rice wine)
- 1 clove garlic, minced
- 1 teaspoon of grated ginger
- 1 tablespoon cornstarch
- 1 tablespoon water
- Sesame seeds, for garnish
- Sliced green onions, for garnish
- Cooked white rice, for serving (optional)

Instructions List

1. In a small bowl, whisk together soy sauce, honey, rice vinegar, mirin, minced garlic, and grated ginger.

2. In a separate bowl, mix cornstarch and water until cornstarch is fully dissolved.

3. Place the salmon pieces in a large bowl. Pour half of the teriyaki sauce over the salmon and toss to coat. Marinate for 10 minutes.

4. Preheat your Emeril Lagasse French Door Large Air Fryer Oven to 400°F.

5. Place the marinated salmon pieces in the air fryer basket or on the air fryer tray in a single layer.

6. Air fry the salmon at 400°F for 8-10 minutes, flipping halfway through, until the salmon is cooked through and edges are slightly caramelized.

7. While the salmon is cooking, heat the remaining teriyaki sauce in a small saucepan over medium heat until it thickens slightly. This will be used as a glaze.

8. Once the salmon bites are cooked, remove them from the air fryer and brush with the thickened teriyaki glaze.

9. Serve the Teriyaki Salmon Bites hot, garnished with sesame seeds and sliced green onions. Serve with cooked white rice if desired.

Nutritional Information (per serving, based on 4 servings)

- Calories: 280
- Protein: 26g
- Total Fats: 10g
- Fiber: 0.5g
- Carbohydrates: 22g

Blackened Red Snapper

Time to Prepare: 10 minutes
Cooking Time: 10 minutes
Number of Servings: 4

Ingredients

- 4 red snapper fillets, skin on (about 6 oz each)
- 2 tablespoons paprika
- 1 tablespoon onion powder
- 1 tablespoon garlic powder
- 1 tablespoon dried thyme
- 1 tablespoon dried oregano
- 1 teaspoon of cayenne pepper (adjust to taste)
- 1 teaspoon of black pepper
- 1 teaspoon of salt
- 2 tablespoons olive oil
- Lemon wedges, for serving
- Fresh parsley, chopped, for garnish

Instructions List

1. In a small bowl, mix together paprika, onion powder, garlic powder, dried thyme, dried oregano, cayenne pepper, black pepper, and salt to create the blackening seasoning.

2. Pat dry the red snapper fillets with paper towels. Rub both sides of each fillet with olive oil.

3. Generously coat each fillet with the blackening seasoning mixture, pressing it gently onto the fish to adhere.

4. Preheat your Emeril Lagasse French Door Large Air Fryer Oven to 400°F.

5. Place the red snapper fillets in the air fryer basket or on the air fryer tray in a single layer.

6. Air fry the red snapper at 400°F for 8-10 minutes, depending on the thickness of the fillets, until the fish is opaque and flakes easily with a fork.

7. Serve the Blackened Red Snapper hot, garnished with lemon wedges and chopped fresh parsley.

Nutritional Information (per serving, based on 4 servings)

- Calories: 255

- Protein: 29g
- Total Fats: 11g
- Fiber: 3g
- Carbohydrates: 5g

Crab Cakes

Time to Prepare: 20 minutes
Cooking Time: 12 minutes
Number of Servings: 4

Ingredients

- 1 lb lump crab meat, picked over for shells
- 1/2 cup of breadcrumbs
- 1/4 cup of mayonnaise
- 1 egg, beaten
- 2 tablespoons Dijon mustard
- 2 tablespoons fresh lemon juice
- 1 tablespoon Worcestershire sauce
- 1 teaspoon of Old Bay seasoning
- 1/4 cup of finely chopped green onions
- 1/4 cup of finely chopped red bell pepper
- 2 tablespoons finely chopped fresh parsley
- 1/2 teaspoon of salt
- 1/2 teaspoon of black pepper
- Olive oil spray

Instructions List

1. In a large bowl, combine the crab meat, breadcrumbs, mayonnaise, egg, Dijon mustard, lemon juice, Worcestershire sauce, Old Bay seasoning, green onions, red bell pepper, parsley, salt, and black pepper. Mix gently to avoid breaking up the crab meat too much.

2. Form the mixture into 8 patties, about 1/2 inch thick.

3. Preheat the Emeril Lagasse French Door Large Air Fryer Oven to 375°F using the Air Fry function.

4. Spray the air fryer basket or tray with olive oil spray. Place the crab cakes in a single layer in the basket or on the tray.

5. Lightly spray the tops of the crab cakes with olive oil spray.

6. Air fry the crab cakes at 375°F for 10-12 minutes, or until they are golden brown and crispy. Flip the crab cakes halfway through cooking for even browning.

7. Remove the crab cakes from the air fryer and let them cool slightly before serving.

8. Serve the crab cakes hot, with lemon wedges and your favorite dipping sauce.

Nutritional Information (per serving, based on 4 servings)

- Calories: 210
- Protein: 20g
- Total Fats: 11g
- Fiber: 1g
- Carbohydrates: 12g

Spicy Tuna Steaks
Time to Prepare: 15 minutes
Cooking Time: 10 minutes
Number of Servings: 2

Ingredients

- 2 tuna steaks (about 6 oz each)
- 1 tablespoon olive oil
- 1 tablespoon soy sauce
- 1 tablespoon Sriracha sauce
- 1 teaspoon of honey
- 1 clove garlic, minced
- 1/2 teaspoon of ground ginger
- 1/2 teaspoon of black pepper
- 1/4 teaspoon of salt
- Lemon wedges (for serving)

Instructions List

1. In a small bowl, mix together olive oil, soy sauce, Sriracha sauce, honey, minced garlic, ground ginger, black pepper, and salt.

2. Place the tuna steaks in a shallow dish and pour the marinade over them, making sure they are well-coated. Let them marinate for at least 15 minutes.

3. Preheat the Emeril Lagasse French Door Large Air Fryer Oven to 400°F using the Broil function.

4. Place the marinated tuna steaks on the air fryer rack.

5. Broil the tuna steaks for 5-6 minutes per side, or until they reach your desired level of doneness.

6. Remove the tuna steaks from the oven and let them rest for a couple of minutes before serving.

7. Serve with lemon wedges on the side.

Nutritional Information (per serving, based on 2 servings)

- Calories: 220
- Protein: 32g
- Total Fats: 9g
- Fiber: 0g
- Carbohydrates: 4g

Air Fried Calamari
Time to Prepare: 20 minutes
Cooking Time: 10 minutes
Number of Servings: 4

Ingredients

- 1 pound calamari rings
- 1 cup of all-purpose flour
- 2 large eggs, beaten
- 1 cup of panko breadcrumbs
- 1/2 teaspoon of paprika
- 1/2 teaspoon of garlic powder
- 1/2 teaspoon of salt

- 1/4 teaspoon of black pepper

- Cooking spray

- Lemon wedges (for serving)

- Marinara sauce (for serving, optional)

Instructions List

1. Preheat the Emeril Lagasse French Door Large Air Fryer Oven to 400°F using the Air Fry function.

2. In a shallow dish, combine the flour, paprika, garlic powder, salt, and black pepper.

3. Place the beaten eggs in another shallow dish.

4. Place the panko breadcrumbs in a third shallow dish.

5. Dredge each calamari ring in the flour mixture, then dip in the beaten eggs, and finally coat with panko breadcrumbs.

6. Arrange the breaded calamari rings in a single layer on the air fryer rack. Spray them lightly with cooking spray.

7. Air fry the calamari for 8-10 minutes, turning halfway through, until golden brown and crispy.

8. Serve with lemon wedges and marinara sauce, if desired.

Nutritional Information (per serving, based on 4 servings)

- Calories: 280

- Protein: 18g

- Total Fats: 8g

- Fiber: 1g

- Carbohydrates: 34g

Chapter 6: Vegetables and Sides

Crispy Brussels Sprouts

Time to Prepare: 10 minutes
Cooking Time: 15 minutes
Number of Servings: 4

Ingredients

- 1 pound Brussels sprouts, trimmed and halved
- 2 tablespoons olive oil
- 1/2 teaspoon of salt
- 1/4 teaspoon of black pepper
- 1/4 teaspoon of garlic powder
- 1/4 teaspoon of smoked paprika
- 1 tablespoon balsamic glaze (optional, for serving)

Instructions List

1. Preheat the Emeril Lagasse French Door Large Air Fryer Oven to 375°F using the Air Fry function.
2. In a large bowl, toss the halved Brussels sprouts with olive oil, salt, black pepper, garlic powder, and smoked paprika until evenly coated.
3. Spread the Brussels sprouts in a single layer on the air fryer rack.
4. Air fry for 12-15 minutes, shaking the basket halfway through, until the Brussels sprouts are crispy and golden brown.
5. Drizzle with balsamic glaze before serving, if desired.

Nutritional Information (per serving, based on 4 servings)

- Calories: 120
- Protein: 3g
- Total Fats: 7g
- Fiber: 4g
- Carbohydrates: 12g

Garlic Parmesan Asparagus

Time to Prepare: 10 minutes
Cooking Time: 10 minutes
Number of Servings: 4

Ingredients

- 1 pound asparagus, trimmed
- 2 tablespoons olive oil
- 3 cloves garlic, minced
- 1/2 teaspoon of salt
- 1/4 teaspoon of black pepper
- 1/4 cup of grated Parmesan cheese
- 1 tablespoon lemon juice (optional, for serving)

Instructions List

1. Preheat the Emeril Lagasse French Door Large Air Fryer Oven to 400°F using the Air Fry function.
2. In a large bowl, toss the asparagus with olive oil, minced garlic, salt, and black pepper until evenly coated.
3. Spread the asparagus in a single layer on the air fryer rack.
4. Air fry for 8-10 minutes, shaking the basket halfway through, until the asparagus is tender and slightly crispy.
5. Remove from the oven and immediately sprinkle with grated Parmesan cheese.
6. Drizzle with lemon juice before serving, if desired.

Nutritional Information (per serving, based on 4 servings)

- Calories: 90
- Protein: 4g
- Total Fats: 7g
- Fiber: 3g
- Carbohydrates: 5g

Sweet Potato Fries

Time to Prepare: 10 minutes
Cooking Time: 15 minutes
Number of Servings: 4

Ingredients

- 2 large sweet potatoes, peeled and cut into fries
- 2 tablespoons olive oil
- 1 teaspoon of paprika
- 1/2 teaspoon of garlic powder
- 1/2 teaspoon of salt
- 1/4 teaspoon of black pepper

Instructions List

1. Preheat the Emeril Lagasse French Door Large Air Fryer Oven to 400°F using the Air Fry function.

2. In a large bowl, toss the sweet potato fries with olive oil, paprika, garlic powder, salt, and black pepper until evenly coated.

3. Spread the fries in a single layer on the air fryer rack.

4. Air fry for 15 minutes, shaking the basket halfway through, until the fries are crispy and golden brown.

5. Remove from the oven and serve immediately.

Nutritional Information (per serving, based on 4 servings)

- Calories: 150
- Protein: 2g
- Total Fats: 7g
- Fiber: 4g
- Carbohydrates: 22g

Air Fried Zucchini Chips

Time to Prepare: 10 minutes
Cooking Time: 15 minutes
Number of Servings: 4

Ingredients

- 2 medium zucchinis, thinly sliced
- 1/2 cup of breadcrumbs
- 1/4 cup of grated Parmesan cheese
- 1/2 teaspoon of garlic powder
- 1/2 teaspoon of paprika
- 1/4 teaspoon of salt
- 1/4 teaspoon of black pepper
- 2 large eggs, beaten

Instructions List

1. Preheat the Emeril Lagasse French Door Large Air Fryer Oven to 400°F using the Air Fry function.

2. In a shallow bowl, mix together breadcrumbs, Parmesan cheese, garlic powder, paprika, salt, and black pepper.

3. Dip each zucchini slice into the beaten eggs, then coat with the breadcrumb mixture.

4. Place the coated zucchini slices in a single layer on the air fryer rack.

5. Air fry for 12-15 minutes, flipping halfway through, until golden and crispy.

6. Remove from the oven and serve immediately.

Nutritional Information (per serving, based on 4 servings)

- Calories: 120
- Protein: 6g
- Total Fats: 5g
- Fiber: 2g
- Carbohydrates: 12g

Roasted Cauliflower

Time to Prepare: 10 minutes
Cooking Time: 25 minutes
Number of Servings: 4

Ingredients

- 1 large head of cauliflower, cut into florets
- 2 tablespoons olive oil

- 1 teaspoon of garlic powder
- 1 teaspoon of paprika
- 1/2 teaspoon of salt
- 1/4 teaspoon of black pepper
- 1/4 cup of grated Parmesan cheese (optional)

Instructions List

1. Preheat the Emeril Lagasse French Door Large Air Fryer Oven to 375°F using the Roast function.

2. In a large bowl, toss the cauliflower florets with olive oil, garlic powder, paprika, salt, and black pepper until evenly coated.

3. Spread the cauliflower florets in a single layer on the air fryer rack.

4. Roast for 20-25 minutes, stirring halfway through, until tender and golden brown.

5. If using, sprinkle Parmesan cheese over the cauliflower during the last 5 minutes of cooking.

6. Remove from the oven and serve immediately.

Nutritional Information (per serving, based on 4 servings)

- Calories: 100
- Protein: 3g
- Total Fats: 7g
- Fiber: 3g
- Carbohydrates: 8g

Stuffed Bell Peppers
Time to Prepare: 15 minutes
Cooking Time: 30 minutes
Number of Servings: 4

Ingredients

- 4 large bell peppers, tops cut off and seeds removed
- 1 lb ground beef
- 1 cup of cooked rice

- 1 small onion, finely chopped
- 1 cup of canned diced tomatoes, drained
- 1 cup of shredded mozzarella cheese
- 1 teaspoon of garlic powder
- 1 teaspoon of dried oregano
- 1 teaspoon of salt
- 1/2 teaspoon of black pepper
- 2 tablespoons olive oil

Instructions List

1. Preheat the Emeril Lagasse French Door Large Air Fryer Oven to 350°F using the Bake function.

2. In a large skillet, heat olive oil over medium heat. Add the chopped onion and cook until softened, about 3 minutes.

3. Add the ground beef, garlic powder, oregano, salt, and black pepper to the skillet. Cook until the beef is browned and cooked through, about 5-7 minutes. Drain any excess fat.

4. Stir in the cooked rice and diced tomatoes. Cook for an additional 2 minutes until heated through.

5. Stuff each bell pepper with the beef mixture, packing it down lightly.

6. Place the stuffed bell peppers in the air fryer oven on a baking sheet.

7. Bake for 25 minutes.

8. Sprinkle the shredded mozzarella cheese on top of the peppers and bake for an additional 5 minutes, or until the cheese is melted and bubbly.

9. Remove from the oven and let cool slightly before serving.

Nutritional Information (per serving, based on 4 servings)

- Calories: 350
- Protein: 22g
- Total Fats: 20g
- Fiber: 4g

- Carbohydrates: 20g

Herb-Roasted Potatoes

Time to Prepare: 10 minutes
Cooking Time: 25 minutes
Number of Servings: 4

Ingredients

- 2 lbs baby potatoes, halved
- 3 tablespoons olive oil
- 1 teaspoon of dried rosemary
- 1 teaspoon of dried thyme
- 1 teaspoon of dried oregano
- 1 teaspoon of garlic powder
- 1 teaspoon of salt
- 1/2 teaspoon of black pepper

Instructions List

1. Preheat the Emeril Lagasse French Door Large Air Fryer Oven to 400°F using the Air Fry function.

2. In a large bowl, combine the halved potatoes, olive oil, rosemary, thyme, oregano, garlic powder, salt, and black pepper. Toss until the potatoes are evenly coated.

3. Spread the potatoes in a single layer on the air fryer basket or tray.

4. Air fry for 25 minutes, shaking the basket halfway through cooking, until the potatoes are golden brown and crispy.

5. Remove from the air fryer and let cool slightly before serving.

Nutritional Information (per serving, based on 4 servings)

- Calories: 200
- Protein: 4g
- Total Fats: 10g
- Fiber: 3g
- Carbohydrates: 26g

Air Fryer Green Beans

Time to Prepare: 10 minutes
Cooking Time: 12 minutes
Number of Servings: 4

Ingredients

- 1 lb fresh green beans, trimmed
- 2 tablespoons olive oil
- 1 teaspoon of garlic powder
- 1/2 teaspoon of salt
- 1/4 teaspoon of black pepper
- Optional: grated Parmesan cheese for serving

Instructions List

1. Preheat the Emeril Lagasse French Door Large Air Fryer Oven to 375°F using the Air Fry function.

2. In a large bowl, toss the trimmed green beans with olive oil, garlic powder, salt, and black pepper until well coated.

3. Arrange the green beans in a single layer in the air fryer basket or on the tray.

4. Air fry for 12 minutes, shaking the basket halfway through cooking, until the green beans are crisp-tender and slightly charred.

5. Remove from the air fryer and transfer to a serving dish. Sprinkle with grated Parmesan cheese if desired.

Nutritional Information (per serving, based on 4 servings)

- Calories: 90
- Protein: 2g
- Total Fats: 7g
- Fiber: 4g
- Carbohydrates: 7g

Grilled Corn on the Cob

Time to Prepare: 10 minutes
Cooking Time: 15 minutes
Number of Servings: 4

Ingredients

- 4 ears of corn, husked

- 2 tablespoons olive oil

- Salt and pepper, to taste

- Optional: butter, herbs, or Parmesan cheese for serving

Instructions List

1. Preheat the Emeril Lagasse French Door Large Air Fryer Oven to 400°F using the Grill function.

2. Rub each ear of corn with olive oil and season with salt and pepper.

3. Place the corn directly on the grill rack or in a grill basket if available.

4. Grill for about 15 minutes, turning occasionally, until the corn kernels are tender and slightly charred.

5. Remove from the grill and serve hot with optional butter, herbs, or Parmesan cheese.

Nutritional Information (per serving, based on 4 servings)

- Calories: 170

- Protein: 4g

- Total Fats: 8g

- Fiber: 3g

- Carbohydrates: 24g

Cheesy Broccoli Bites
Time to Prepare: 15 minutes
Cooking Time: 15 minutes
Number of Servings: 4

Ingredients

- 2 cups of broccoli florets, finely chopped

- 1 cup of shredded cheddar cheese

- 1/2 cup of breadcrumbs

- 1/4 cup of grated Parmesan cheese

- 2 large eggs

- 1/2 teaspoon of garlic powder

- Salt and pepper, to taste

- Cooking spray or olive oil

Instructions List

1. Preheat the Emeril Lagasse French Door Large Air Fryer Oven to 375°F using the Air Fry function.

2. In a large bowl, combine the chopped broccoli, cheddar cheese, breadcrumbs, Parmesan cheese, eggs, garlic powder, salt, and pepper. Mix until well mixed.

3. Form the mixture into small bite-sized balls or patties.

4. Lightly coat the air fryer basket with cooking spray or brush with olive oil.

5. Arrange the broccoli bites in a single layer in the air fryer basket.

6. Air fry at 375°F for about 15 minutes, flipping halfway through, until the bites are golden brown and crispy.

7. Remove from the air fryer and let cool slightly before serving.

Nutritional Information (per serving, based on 4 servings)

- Calories: 250

- Protein: 14g

- Total Fats: 15g

- Fiber: 4g

- Carbohydrates: 18g

Honey Glazed Carrots
Time to Prepare: 10 minutes
Cooking Time: 20 minutes
Number of Servings: 4

Ingredients

- 1 lb (450g) carrots, peeled and sliced into thin rounds

- 2 tablespoons honey

- 2 tablespoons unsalted butter, melted

- 1/2 teaspoon of ground cinnamon

- Salt and pepper, to taste

- Chopped fresh parsley (optional, for garnish)

Instructions List

1. Preheat the Emeril Lagasse French Door Large Air Fryer Oven to 375°F using the Roast function.

2. In a bowl, combine the sliced carrots, honey, melted butter, ground cinnamon, salt, and pepper. Toss until the carrots are evenly coated.

3. Transfer the honey glazed carrots to a baking sheet lined with parchment paper or directly into the air fryer basket.

4. Roast at 375°F for about 20 minutes, shaking the basket halfway through, until the carrots are tender and caramelized.

5. Remove from the oven or air fryer and transfer to a serving dish.

6. Garnish with chopped fresh parsley, if desired, and serve hot.

Nutritional Information (per serving, based on 4 servings)

- Calories: 130
- Protein: 1g
- Total Fats: 5g
- Fiber: 4g
- Carbohydrates: 22g

Baked Eggplant Parmesan

Time to Prepare: 30 minutes
Cooking Time: 30 minutes
Number of Servings: 4

Ingredients

- 1 large eggplant, sliced into 1/2-inch rounds
- 1 cup of breadcrumbs (preferably seasoned)
- 1/2 cup of grated Parmesan cheese
- 2 eggs, beaten
- 1 cup of marinara sauce
- 1 cup of shredded mozzarella cheese
- Fresh basil leaves, chopped (for garnish)

- Salt and pepper, to taste
- Olive oil spray

Instructions List

1. Preheat the Emeril Lagasse French Door Large Air Fryer Oven to 375°F using the Bake function.

2. Season eggplant slices with salt and pepper. Dip each slice into beaten eggs, then coat with breadcrumbs mixed with Parmesan cheese.

3. Place the coated eggplant slices on a baking sheet lined with parchment paper or directly into the air fryer basket, ensuring they are in a single layer. Lightly spray or brush with olive oil.

4. Bake at 375°F for about 20 minutes, flipping halfway through, until golden brown and crispy.

5. Remove the eggplant slices from the oven or air fryer and lower the temperature to 350°F.

6. In a baking dish or oven-safe pan, spread a thin layer of marinara sauce. Arrange half of the baked eggplant slices over the sauce.

7. Top with more marinara sauce and half of the shredded mozzarella cheese.

8. Repeat with another layer of eggplant, marinara sauce, and mozzarella cheese.

9. Bake at 350°F for an additional 10 minutes, or until the cheese is melted and bubbly.

10. Remove from the oven and let it rest for a few minutes. Garnish with chopped fresh basil before serving.

Nutritional Information (per serving, based on 4 servings)

- Calories: 350
- Protein: 18g
- Total Fats: 18g
- Fiber: 8g
- Carbohydrates: 30g

Crispy Onion Rings

Time to Prepare: 20 minutes
Cooking Time: 10 minutes
Number of Servings: 4

Ingredients

- 2 large onions, cut into 1/4-inch thick rings
- 1 cup of all-purpose flour
- 1 teaspoon of garlic powder
- 1 teaspoon of paprika
- 1/2 teaspoon of salt
- 1/4 teaspoon of black pepper
- 2 eggs, beaten
- 1 cup of Panko breadcrumbs
- Olive oil spray

Instructions List

1. Preheat the Emeril Lagasse French Door Large Air Fryer Oven to 400°F using the Air Fry function.

2. In a shallow bowl, combine flour, garlic powder, paprika, salt, and black pepper.

3. Dip each onion ring into the flour mixture, shaking off any excess.

4. Dip the flour-coated onion rings into the beaten eggs, allowing any excess egg to drip off.

5. Coat the onion rings with Panko breadcrumbs, pressing gently to adhere.

6. Place the coated onion rings in a single layer on the air fryer basket or tray. Lightly spray with olive oil.

7. Air fry at 400°F for 5 minutes. Flip the onion rings, lightly spray with olive oil again, and air fry for an additional 5 minutes or until golden brown and crispy.

8. Remove the onion rings from the air fryer and serve immediately.

Nutritional Information (per serving, based on 4 servings)

- Calories: 240
- Protein: 7g
- Total Fats: 6g
- Fiber: 3g
- Carbohydrates: 40g

Roasted Beet Salad

Time to Prepare: 15 minutes
Cooking Time: 45 minutes
Number of Servings: 4

Ingredients

- 4 medium beets, peeled and cut into 1/2-inch cubes
- 2 tablespoons olive oil
- Salt and pepper, to taste
- 4 cups of mixed salad greens
- 1/4 cup of crumbled feta cheese
- 1/4 cup of walnuts, toasted
- Balsamic glaze, for drizzling

Instructions List

1. Preheat the Emeril Lagasse French Door Large Air Fryer Oven to 400°F using the Roast function.

2. In a bowl, toss the cubed beets with olive oil, salt, and pepper until evenly coated.

3. Spread the seasoned beets in a single layer on a baking sheet or air fryer tray.

4. Roast the beets in the preheated oven for 40-45 minutes, tossing halfway through, until tender and slightly caramelized.

5. Remove the roasted beets from the oven and let them cool slightly.

6. In a large bowl, combine the roasted beets with mixed salad greens, crumbled feta cheese, and toasted walnuts.

7. Drizzle with balsamic glaze and toss gently to combine.

8. Serve the roasted beet salad immediately.

Nutritional Information (per serving, based on 4 servings)

- Calories: 220

- Protein: 6g

- Total Fats: 15g

- Fiber: 5g

- Carbohydrates: 18g

Air Fryer Stuffed Tomatoes

Time to Prepare: 15 minutes
Cooking Time: 15 minutes
Number of Servings: 4

Ingredients

- 4 large tomatoes

- 1 cup of cooked quinoa

- 1/2 cup of crumbled feta cheese

- 1/4 cup of chopped fresh parsley

- 2 cloves garlic, minced

- 1 tablespoon olive oil

- Salt and pepper, to taste

- Fresh basil leaves, for garnish (optional)

Instructions List

1. Preheat the Emeril Lagasse French Door Large Air Fryer Oven to 375°F using the Air Fry function.

2. Cut the tops off the tomatoes and scoop out the seeds and pulp to create hollow shells. Reserve the pulp.

3. In a bowl, combine the cooked quinoa, crumbled feta cheese, chopped parsley, minced garlic, olive oil, salt, and pepper. Mix well.

4. Stuff each tomato with the quinoa mixture, packing it firmly.

5. Place the stuffed tomatoes in the air fryer basket or on the air fryer tray.

6. Air fry the stuffed tomatoes at 375°F for 12-15 minutes until the tomatoes are tender and the filling is heated through and lightly browned on top.

7. Remove the stuffed tomatoes from the air fryer and garnish with fresh basil leaves if desired.

8. Serve the air fryer stuffed tomatoes warm.

Nutritional Information (per serving, based on 4 servings)

- Calories: 180

- Protein: 6g

- Total Fats: 8g

- Fiber: 4g

- Carbohydrates: 22g

Chapter 7: Vegan

Air Fryer Tofu Stir-Fry

Time to Prepare: 20 minutes
Cooking Time: 20 minutes
Number of Servings: 4

Ingredients

- 1 block (14 oz) firm tofu, drained and pressed
- 2 tablespoons soy sauce
- 2 tablespoons cornstarch
- 2 tablespoons vegetable oil
- 1 red bell pepper, thinly sliced
- 1 yellow bell pepper, thinly sliced
- 1 green bell pepper, thinly sliced
- 1 cup of snap peas
- 3 cloves garlic, minced
- 1 tablespoon minced ginger
- 1/4 cup of soy sauce
- 2 tablespoons hoisin sauce
- 1 tablespoon rice vinegar
- 1 tablespoon sesame oil
- 2 green onions, chopped (for garnish)
- Sesame seeds (for garnish)
- Cooked rice, for serving

Instructions List

1. Preheat the Emeril Lagasse French Door Large Air Fryer Oven to 400°F using the Air Fry function.

2. Cut the tofu into 1-inch cubes. In a bowl, toss the tofu cubes with 2 tablespoons of soy sauce and cornstarch until evenly coated.

3. Place the tofu cubes in the air fryer basket in a single layer. Air fry at 400°F for 15-20 minutes, shaking the basket halfway through, until the tofu is crispy and golden brown.

4. While the tofu is cooking, heat vegetable oil in a large skillet over medium-high heat. Add the sliced bell peppers and snap peas. Stir-fry for 5-6 minutes until the vegetables are tender-crisp.

5. Add minced garlic and ginger to the skillet. Stir-fry for another 1-2 minutes until fragrant.

6. In a small bowl, whisk together 1/4 cup of soy sauce, hoisin sauce, rice vinegar, and sesame oil.

7. Add the air fried tofu cubes to the skillet with the vegetables. Pour the sauce over the tofu and vegetables. Stir well to coat everything evenly.

8. Cook for another 1-2 minutes until the sauce thickens slightly and coats the tofu and vegetables.

9. Remove from heat and garnish with chopped green onions and sesame seeds.

10. Serve the tofu stir-fry immediately over cooked rice.

Nutritional Information (per serving, based on 4 servings)

- Calories: 320
- Protein: 14g
- Total Fats: 18g
- Fiber: 6g
- Carbohydrates: 30g

Quinoa and Veggie Bowls

Time to Prepare: 15 minutes
Cooking Time: 30 minutes
Number of Servings: 4

Ingredients

- 1 cup of quinoa, rinsed
- 2 cups of water or vegetable broth
- 1 tablespoon olive oil
- 1 red bell pepper, diced

- 1 yellow bell pepper, diced

- 1 zucchini, diced

- 1 yellow squash, diced

- 1 cup of cherry tomatoes, halved

- 1 teaspoon of garlic powder

- 1 teaspoon of smoked paprika

- Salt and pepper, to taste

- 1 avocado, sliced (for serving)

- Fresh cilantro or parsley, chopped (for garnish)

Instructions List

1. **Cook Quinoa:**

   o In a saucepan, combine quinoa and water or vegetable broth. Bring to a boil, then reduce heat to low, cover, and simmer for 15 minutes or until quinoa is cooked and liquid is absorbed. Fluff with a fork and set aside.

2. **Prepare Vegetables:**

   o Preheat the Emeril Lagasse French Door Large Air Fryer Oven to 400°F using the Air Fry function.

   o In a large bowl, toss diced red bell pepper, yellow bell pepper, zucchini, yellow squash, and cherry tomatoes with olive oil, garlic powder, smoked paprika, salt, and pepper until evenly coated.

3. **Air Fry Vegetables:**

   o Place the seasoned vegetables in the air fryer basket in a single layer.

   o Air fry at 400°F for 15-20 minutes, shaking the basket halfway through, until the vegetables are tender and slightly charred.

4. **Assemble Bowls:**

   o Divide cooked quinoa among serving bowls.

   o Top with air fried vegetables.

5. **Serve:**

   o Garnish with sliced avocado and chopped cilantro or parsley.

Nutritional Information (per serving, based on 4 servings)

- Calories: 320

- Protein: 8g

- Total Fats: 12g

- Fiber: 10g

- Carbohydrates: 45g

Air Fried Cauliflower Steaks

Time to Prepare: 10 minutes
Cooking Time: 20 minutes
Number of Servings: 2

Ingredients

- 1 head cauliflower

- 2 tablespoons olive oil

- 1 teaspoon of garlic powder

- 1 teaspoon of paprika

- Salt and pepper, to taste

- Fresh parsley, chopped (for garnish)

Instructions List

1. **Prepare Cauliflower:**

   o Remove the leaves from the cauliflower and trim the stem, keeping the core intact. Slice the cauliflower into 1-inch thick steaks. You should get about 2 steaks from one head of cauliflower.

2. **Seasoning:**

   o In a small bowl, mix together olive oil, garlic powder, paprika, salt, and pepper.

3. **Coat Cauliflower:**

   o Brush both sides of each cauliflower steak with the seasoned olive oil mixture, ensuring they are well coated.

4. **Preheat Air Fryer:**

o Preheat the Emeril Lagasse French Door Large Air Fryer Oven to 400°F using the Air Fry function.

5. **Air Fry Cauliflower Steaks:**

   o Place the cauliflower steaks in the air fryer basket in a single layer.

   o Air fry at 400°F for 10 minutes. Flip the steaks and air fry for an additional 8-10 minutes, or until the cauliflower is tender and golden brown.

6. **Serve:**

   o Transfer the cauliflower steaks to a serving plate.

   o Garnish with chopped fresh parsley.

Nutritional Information (per serving, based on 2 servings)

- Calories: 180
- Protein: 5g
- Total Fats: 14g
- Fiber: 5g
- Carbohydrates: 12g

Vegan Stuffed Peppers

Time to Prepare: 20 minutes
Cooking Time: 25 minutes
Number of Servings: 4

Ingredients

- 4 large bell peppers (any color)
- 1 cup of quinoa, rinsed
- 1 3/4 cups of vegetable broth
- 1 tablespoon olive oil
- 1 small onion, diced
- 2 cloves garlic, minced
- 1 can (15 ounces) black beans, drained and rinsed
- 1 cup of corn kernels (fresh or frozen)
- 1 teaspoon of ground cumin
- 1 teaspoon of chili powder
- Salt and pepper, to taste
- 1/2 cup of shredded vegan cheese (optional)
- Fresh cilantro or parsley, chopped (for garnish)

Instructions List

1. **Prepare Bell Peppers:**

   o Cut the tops off the bell peppers and remove the seeds and membranes. Set aside.

2. **Cook Quinoa:**

   o In a saucepan, combine quinoa and vegetable broth. Bring to a boil, then reduce heat to low, cover, and simmer for 15 minutes or until quinoa is cooked and broth is absorbed.

3. **Sauté Onion and Garlic:**

   o While quinoa is cooking, heat olive oil in a skillet over medium heat. Add diced onion and sauté until translucent, about 3-4 minutes. Add minced garlic and cook for another 1 minute until fragrant.

4. **Combine Ingredients:**

   o In a large bowl, combine cooked quinoa, sautéed onion and garlic, black beans, corn kernels, ground cumin, chili powder, salt, and pepper. Mix well to combine.

5. **Preheat Air Fryer:**

   o Preheat the Emeril Lagasse French Door Large Air Fryer Oven to 375°F using the Bake function.

6. **Stuff Peppers:**

   o Stuff each bell pepper with the quinoa mixture, pressing down gently to fill completely. Place stuffed peppers in a baking dish or directly on the air fryer tray.

7. **Bake:**

   o Place the stuffed peppers in the preheated air fryer oven.

- o Bake at 375°F for 20-25 minutes, or until the peppers are tender and the filling is heated through.

8. **Serve:**

- o If desired, sprinkle shredded vegan cheese over the stuffed peppers during the last 5 minutes of baking.

- o Garnish with chopped cilantro or parsley before serving.

Nutritional Information (per serving, based on 4 servings)

- Calories: 380
- Protein: 15g
- Total Fats: 8g
- Fiber: 12g
- Carbohydrates: 65g

Crispy Chickpea Snacks

Time to Prepare: 10 minutes
Cooking Time: 20 minutes
Number of Servings: 4

Ingredients

- 2 cans (15 ounces each) chickpeas, drained, rinsed, and patted dry
- 1 tablespoon olive oil
- 1 teaspoon of ground cumin
- 1 teaspoon of smoked paprika
- 1/2 teaspoon of garlic powder
- 1/2 teaspoon of salt
- 1/4 teaspoon of cayenne pepper (optional, for added heat)
- Cooking spray (for greasing the air fryer basket)

Instructions List

1. **Preheat Air Fryer:**

- o Preheat the Emeril Lagasse French Door Large Air Fryer Oven to 400°F using the Air Fry function.

2. **Prepare Chickpeas:**

- o In a large bowl, toss the chickpeas with olive oil, ground cumin, smoked paprika, garlic powder, salt, and cayenne pepper (if using), ensuring the chickpeas are evenly coated.

3. **Air Fry Chickpeas:**

- o Lightly grease the air fryer basket with cooking spray.

- o Spread the seasoned chickpeas in an even layer in the air fryer basket.

4. **Cook Chickpeas:**

- o Air fry at 400°F for 15-20 minutes, shaking the basket halfway through cooking, until the chickpeas are crispy and golden brown.

5. **Cool and Serve:**

- o Remove chickpeas from the air fryer and let them cool slightly before serving.

Nutritional Information (per serving, based on 4 servings)

- Calories: 240
- Protein: 10g
- Total Fats: 8g
- Fiber: 10g
- Carbohydrates: 34g

Sweet Potato and Black Bean Tacos

Time to Prepare: 15 minutes
Cooking Time: 30 minutes
Number of Servings: 4

Ingredients

- 2 medium sweet potatoes, peeled and diced
- 1 tablespoon olive oil
- 1 teaspoon of ground cumin
- 1 teaspoon of chili powder
- Salt and pepper, to taste
- 1 can (15 ounces) black beans, drained and rinsed

- 1 cup of corn kernels (fresh or frozen)
- 1/2 red onion, diced
- 1 bell pepper (any color), diced
- 1 teaspoon of minced garlic
- 8 small corn tortillas
- Optional toppings: avocado, salsa, cilantro, lime wedges

Instructions List

1. **Preheat Oven:**

   o Preheat the Emeril Lagasse French Door Large Air Fryer Oven to 400°F using the Bake function.

2. **Roast Sweet Potatoes:**

   o In a bowl, toss diced sweet potatoes with olive oil, ground cumin, chili powder, salt, and pepper.

   o Spread the seasoned sweet potatoes on a baking sheet lined with parchment paper.

   o Roast in the preheated oven for 20-25 minutes, until tender and lightly browned, flipping halfway through.

3. **Prepare Filling:**

   o In a skillet, heat a drizzle of olive oil over medium heat.

   o Add diced onion, bell pepper, and minced garlic. Cook until softened, about 5 minutes.

   o Add black beans and corn kernels. Cook for another 3-4 minutes, until heated through. Season with salt and pepper to taste.

4. **Assemble Tacos:**

   o Warm the corn tortillas in the oven or microwave until soft and pliable.

   o Fill each tortilla with roasted sweet potatoes and the black bean-corn mixture.

5. **Serve:**

   o Serve the tacos hot, topped with optional toppings such as avocado

slices, salsa, cilantro, and a squeeze of lime juice.

Nutritional Information (per serving, based on 4 servings)

- Calories: 350
- Protein: 10g
- Total Fats: 7g
- Fiber: 10g
- Carbohydrates: 65g

Air Fryer Falafel

Time to Prepare: 15 minutes
Cooking Time: 15 minutes
Number of Servings: 4

Ingredients

- 1 can (15 ounces) chickpeas, drained and rinsed
- 1/2 small red onion, chopped
- 2 cloves garlic, minced
- 1/4 cup of fresh parsley, chopped
- 1/4 cup of fresh cilantro, chopped
- 1 teaspoon of ground cumin
- 1 teaspoon of ground coriander
- 1/2 teaspoon of salt
- 1/4 teaspoon of black pepper
- 2 tablespoons all-purpose flour or chickpea flour
- 1 tablespoon lemon juice
- 1 tablespoon olive oil
- Cooking spray or olive oil spray

Instructions List

1. **Preheat Oven:**

   o Preheat the Emeril Lagasse French Door Large Air Fryer Oven to 375°F using the Air Fryer function.

2. **Prepare Falafel Mixture:**

- o In a food processor, combine chickpeas, red onion, garlic, parsley, cilantro, cumin, coriander, salt, pepper, flour, lemon juice, and olive oil.

- o Pulse until the mixture comes together but still has some texture. You may need to scrape down the sides of the processor bowl as needed.

3. **Form Falafel Patties:**

- o Form the mixture into small patties or balls, about 1.5 inches in diameter.

4. **Air Fry Falafel:**

- o Lightly coat the air fryer basket with cooking spray or brush with olive oil.

- o Arrange falafel patties in a single layer in the air fryer basket, leaving space between them.

- o Air fry at 375°F for 12-15 minutes, flipping halfway through, until falafel are golden brown and crispy.

5. **Serve:**

- o Serve falafel warm with pita bread, hummus, tahini sauce, and your favorite salad or vegetables.

Nutritional Information (per serving, based on 4 servings)

- Calories: 220
- Protein: 9g
- Total Fats: 8g
- Fiber: 6g
- Carbohydrates: 29g

Grilled Portobello Mushrooms

Time to Prepare: 10 minutes
Cooking Time: 10 minutes
Number of Servings: 2

Ingredients

- 2 large Portobello mushrooms, stems removed

- 2 tablespoons balsamic vinegar
- 2 tablespoons olive oil
- 2 cloves garlic, minced
- 1/2 teaspoon of dried thyme
- Salt and pepper, to taste
- Cooking spray or olive oil spray

Instructions List

1. **Marinate Mushrooms:**

- o In a small bowl, whisk together balsamic vinegar, olive oil, minced garlic, dried thyme, salt, and pepper.

2. **Prepare Mushrooms:**

- o Place Portobello mushrooms in a shallow dish or resealable plastic bag. Pour the marinade over the mushrooms, making sure they are well coated. Marinate for at least 10 minutes, turning once.

3. **Preheat Oven:**

- o Preheat the Emeril Lagasse French Door Large Air Fryer Oven to 375°F using the Grill function.

4. **Grill Mushrooms:**

- o Lightly coat the air fryer basket or grill rack with cooking spray or brush with olive oil.

- o Place the marinated Portobello mushrooms in the air fryer basket or on the grill rack, gill side up.

- o Grill at 375°F for 8-10 minutes, depending on the size of the mushrooms and desired doneness, flipping halfway through.

5. **Serve:**

- o Serve grilled Portobello mushrooms hot, optionally topped with additional fresh herbs or a drizzle of balsamic glaze.

Nutritional Information (per serving, based on 2 servings)

- Calories: 150

- Protein: 4g
- Total Fats: 12g
- Fiber: 2g
- Carbohydrates: 9g

Air Fryer Avocado Tacos

Time to Prepare: 15 minutes
Cooking Time: 10 minutes
Number of Servings: 2

Ingredients

- 2 ripe avocados
- 1 cup of panko breadcrumbs
- 1 teaspoon of chili powder
- 1/2 teaspoon of cumin
- 1/2 teaspoon of paprika
- Salt and pepper, to taste
- 1 egg, beaten
- Cooking spray or olive oil spray
- 4 small tortillas (corn or flour)
- Optional toppings: shredded lettuce, diced tomatoes, salsa, sour cream

Instructions List

1. **Prepare Avocados:**
   - Peel and pit the avocados. Slice each avocado into thick wedges.

2. **Prepare Breadcrumb Mixture:**
   - In a shallow bowl, combine panko breadcrumbs, chili powder, cumin, paprika, salt, and pepper.

3. **Coat Avocado Slices:**
   - Dip each avocado slice into the beaten egg, then coat evenly with the breadcrumb mixture, pressing gently to adhere.

4. **Preheat Oven:**
   - Preheat the Emeril Lagasse French Door Large Air Fryer Oven to 375°F using the Air Fry function.

5. **Air Fry Avocado Slices:**
   - Lightly coat the air fryer basket with cooking spray or brush with olive oil.
   - Arrange the breaded avocado slices in a single layer in the air fryer basket.
   - Air fry at 375°F for 8-10 minutes, flipping halfway through, until golden brown and crispy.

6. **Warm Tortillas:**
   - While the avocado slices are air frying, warm the tortillas in the air fryer for 1-2 minutes until heated through.

7. **Assemble Tacos:**
   - Place a few avocado slices on each tortilla.
   - Add optional toppings such as shredded lettuce, diced tomatoes, salsa, or sour cream.

8. **Serve:**
   - Serve the air fryer avocado tacos immediately while warm.

Nutritional Information (per serving, based on 2 servings)

- Calories: 470
- Protein: 10g
- Total Fats: 26g
- Fiber: 12g
- Carbohydrates: 54g

Vegan Eggplant Fries

Time to Prepare: 20 minutes
Cooking Time: 15 minutes
Number of Servings: 4

Ingredients

- 1 large eggplant
- 1 cup of panko breadcrumbs
- 1/2 cup of nutritional yeast

- 1 teaspoon of garlic powder
- 1 teaspoon of onion powder
- 1/2 teaspoon of paprika
- Salt and pepper, to taste
- Cooking spray or olive oil spray
- Marinara sauce or vegan ranch dressing, for dipping

Instructions List

1. **Prepare Eggplant:**
   - Wash the eggplant and cut it into fry-shaped sticks, about 1/2-inch thick.

2. **Prepare Breadcrumb Mixture:**
   - In a shallow bowl, combine panko breadcrumbs, nutritional yeast, garlic powder, onion powder, paprika, salt, and pepper.

3. **Coat Eggplant Fries:**
   - Dip each eggplant fry into the breadcrumb mixture, pressing gently to coat evenly.

4. **Preheat Oven:**
   - Preheat the Emeril Lagasse French Door Large Air Fryer Oven to 375°F using the Air Fry function.

5. **Air Fry Eggplant Fries:**
   - Lightly coat the air fryer basket with cooking spray or brush with olive oil.
   - Arrange the breaded eggplant fries in a single layer in the air fryer basket.
   - Air fry at 375°F for 12-15 minutes, shaking the basket halfway through, until the fries are golden brown and crispy.

6. **Serve:**
   - Serve the vegan eggplant fries hot with marinara sauce or vegan ranch dressing for dipping.

Nutritional Information (per serving, based on 4 servings)

- Calories: 210
- Protein: 7g
- Total Fats: 4g
- Fiber: 9g
- Carbohydrates: 38g

Roasted Garlic Brussels Sprouts

Time to Prepare: 10 minutes
Cooking Time: 20 minutes
Number of Servings: 4

Ingredients

- 1 lb Brussels sprouts, trimmed and halved
- 2 tablespoons olive oil
- 4 cloves garlic, minced
- Salt and pepper, to taste
- Optional: grated Parmesan cheese for serving

Instructions List

1. **Prepare Brussels Sprouts:**
   - Preheat the Emeril Lagasse French Door Large Air Fryer Oven to 400°F using the Roast function.

2. **Toss with Olive Oil and Garlic:**
   - In a large bowl, toss the Brussels sprouts with olive oil, minced garlic, salt, and pepper until evenly coated.

3. **Roast in Air Fryer:**
   - Place the Brussels sprouts in a single layer on the air fryer tray or a baking sheet lined with parchment paper.
   - Roast in the preheated oven at 400°F for about 20 minutes, or until the Brussels sprouts are tender and caramelized, stirring halfway through cooking.

4. **Serve:**
   - Transfer the roasted Brussels sprouts to a serving dish.
   - If desired, sprinkle with grated Parmesan cheese before serving.

Nutritional Information (per serving, based on 4 servings)

- Calories: 120
- Protein: 4g
- Total Fats: 7g
- Fiber: 4g
- Carbohydrates: 14g

Balsamic Glazed Carrots
Time to Prepare: 10 minutes
Cooking Time: 20 minutes
Number of Servings: 4

Ingredients

- 1 lb carrots, peeled and cut into sticks or coins
- 2 tablespoons olive oil
- 2 tablespoons balsamic vinegar
- 1 tablespoon honey (optional, adjust to taste)
- Salt and pepper, to taste
- Fresh parsley or thyme for garnish (optional)

Instructions List

1. **Prepare Carrots:**
   o Preheat the Emeril Lagasse French Door Large Air Fryer Oven to 375°F using the Roast function.
2. **Coat Carrots:**
   o In a large bowl, toss the carrots with olive oil, balsamic vinegar, honey (if using), salt, and pepper until evenly coated.
3. **Roast in Air Fryer:**
   o Arrange the carrots in a single layer on the air fryer tray or a baking sheet lined with parchment paper.
   o Roast in the preheated oven at 375°F for about 20 minutes, or until the carrots are tender and caramelized, stirring halfway through cooking.
4. **Glaze and Serve:**

   o Once roasted, remove the carrots from the oven.
   o Drizzle any remaining glaze from the pan over the carrots.
   o Garnish with fresh parsley or thyme if desired.

Nutritional Information (per serving, based on 4 servings)

- Calories: 110
- Protein: 1g
- Total Fats: 7g
- Fiber: 4g
- Carbohydrates: 13g

Vegan Stuffed Mushrooms
Time to Prepare: 15 minutes
Cooking Time: 20 minutes
Number of Servings: 4

Ingredients

- 16 large mushrooms, cleaned and stems removed
- 1 cup of breadcrumbs (preferably whole wheat)
- 1/2 cup of finely chopped onion
- 1/2 cup of finely chopped bell pepper (any color)
- 2 cloves garlic, minced
- 1/4 cup of chopped fresh parsley
- 1/4 cup of nutritional yeast
- 2 tablespoons olive oil
- 1 tablespoon soy sauce or tamari
- Salt and pepper, to taste
- Cooking spray or olive oil for greasing

Instructions List

1. **Prepare Mushrooms:**
   o Preheat the Emeril Lagasse French Door Large Air Fryer Oven to 375°F using the Air Fry function.

2. **Prepare Filling:**

   o   In a bowl, combine breadcrumbs, onion, bell pepper, garlic, parsley, nutritional yeast, olive oil, soy sauce or tamari, salt, and pepper. Mix well until mixed.

3. **Stuff Mushrooms:**

   o   Using a spoon, fill each mushroom cap with the breadcrumb mixture, pressing gently to pack it in.

4. **Air Fry Stuffed Mushrooms:**

   o   Lightly grease the air fryer basket or tray with cooking spray or olive oil.

   o   Arrange the stuffed mushrooms in a single layer in the air fryer basket or on the tray.

   o   Air fry at 375°F for about 15-20 minutes, or until the mushrooms are tender and the filling is golden brown and crisp.

5. **Serve:**

   o   Remove the stuffed mushrooms from the air fryer and let them cool slightly before serving.

   o   Optionally, garnish with additional chopped parsley before serving.

Nutritional Information (per serving, based on 4 servings)

• Calories: 230

• Protein: 8g

• Total Fats: 10g

• Fiber: 5g

• Carbohydrates: 28g

Air Fried Plantains

Time to Prepare: 10 minutes
Cooking Time: 15 minutes
Number of Servings: 4

Ingredients

• 2 ripe plantains

• Cooking spray or oil for greasing

• Optional: salt or cinnamon sugar for sprinkling

Instructions List

1. **Preheat the Air Fryer:**

   o   Preheat the Emeril Lagasse French Door Large Air Fryer Oven to 375°F using the Air Fry function.

2. **Prepare Plantains:**

   o   Peel the plantains and cut them into slices about 1/2 inch thick.

3. **Air Fry Plantains:**

   o   Lightly grease the air fryer basket or tray with cooking spray or oil.

   o   Arrange the plantain slices in a single layer in the air fryer basket or on the tray.

   o   Air fry at 375°F for about 12-15 minutes, flipping halfway through, until the plantains are golden brown and crispy.

4. **Serve:**

   o   Remove the air fried plantains from the air fryer and let them cool slightly before serving.

   o   Optionally, sprinkle with salt or cinnamon sugar for added flavor.

Nutritional Information (per serving, based on 4 servings)

• Calories: 120

• Protein: 1g

• Total Fats: 0.5g

• Fiber: 2g

• Carbohydrates: 31g

Chapter 8: Desserts & Snacks

Air Fryer Donuts

Time to Prepare: 20 minutes
Cooking Time: 8 minutes
Number of Servings: 6

Ingredients

- 1 can (16.3 oz) refrigerated biscuits (8 count)
- 2 tablespoons unsalted butter, melted
- 1/2 cup of granulated sugar
- 1 teaspoon of ground cinnamon

Instructions List

1. **Preheat the Air Fryer:**

   o Preheat the Emeril Lagasse French Door Large Air Fryer Oven to 350°F using the Air Fry function.

2. **Prepare the Donuts:**

   o Remove the biscuits from the can and separate them.

   o Flatten each biscuit into a circle using your hands or a rolling pin.

   o Use a small round cookie cutter or the cap of a bottle to cut out a hole in the center of each biscuit to form a donut shape.

3. **Air Fry the Donuts:**

   o Lightly grease the air fryer basket or tray with cooking spray or brush with melted butter.

   o Arrange the donuts in a single layer in the air fryer basket or on the tray, leaving space between them.

   o Air fry at 350°F for 4 minutes.

4. **Flip and Air Fry Again:**

   o Carefully flip the donuts using tongs or a fork.

   o Air fry for an additional 3-4 minutes, until the donuts are golden brown and cooked through.

5. **Coat with Cinnamon Sugar:**

   o While the donuts are still warm, brush them with melted butter.

   o In a shallow bowl, combine the granulated sugar and ground cinnamon.

   o Dip each donut into the cinnamon sugar mixture, coating all sides evenly.

6. **Serve:**

   o Serve the air fryer donuts warm.

Nutritional Information (per serving, based on 6 servings)

- Calories: 240
- Protein: 3g
- Total Fats: 12g
- Fiber: 1g
- Carbohydrates: 32g

Cinnamon Sugar Churros

Time to Prepare: 15 minutes
Cooking Time: 10 minutes
Number of Servings: 4

Ingredients

- 1 cup of water
- 2 tablespoons granulated sugar
- 1/2 teaspoon of salt
- 2 tablespoons vegetable oil
- 1 cup of all-purpose flour
- 1/4 cup of unsalted butter, melted
- 1/2 cup of granulated sugar (for coating)
- 1 teaspoon of ground cinnamon

Instructions List

1. **Preheat the Air Fryer:**

   o Preheat the Emeril Lagasse French Door Large Air Fryer Oven to 375°F using the Air Fry function.

2. **Prepare the Churro Dough:**

   o In a saucepan over medium heat, combine water, sugar, salt, and vegetable oil. Bring to a boil.

   o Remove from heat and stir in the flour until the mixture forms a ball of dough.

3. **Shape and Fry the Churros:**

   o Spoon the churro dough into a piping bag fitted with a large star tip.

   o Pipe 4-inch long strips of dough onto a greased air fryer tray or basket.

4. **Air Fry the Churros:**

   o Air fry at 375°F for 8-10 minutes, or until the churros are golden brown and crisp.

5. **Coat with Cinnamon Sugar:**

   o In a shallow bowl, combine the granulated sugar and ground cinnamon.

   o Brush the hot churros with melted butter, then roll them in the cinnamon sugar mixture to coat evenly.

6. **Serve:**

   o Serve the cinnamon sugar churros warm.

Nutritional Information (per serving, based on 4 servings)

- Calories: 367

- Protein: 3g

- Total Fats: 18g

- Fiber: 1g

- Carbohydrates: 50g

Chocolate Lava Cakes

Time to Prepare: 15 minutes
Cooking Time: 10 minutes
Number of Servings: 4

Ingredients

- 4 ounces semi-sweet chocolate, chopped

- 1/2 cup of unsalted butter

- 1/2 cup of powdered sugar

- 2 large eggs

- 2 large egg yolks

- 1 teaspoon of vanilla extract

- 1/4 cup of all-purpose flour

- Pinch of salt

- Cooking spray or butter, for greasing

Instructions List

1. **Preheat the Air Fryer:**

   o Preheat the Emeril Lagasse French Door Large Air Fryer Oven to 375°F using the Bake function.

2. **Prepare the Ramekins:**

   o Grease four ramekins with cooking spray or butter.

3. **Melt Chocolate and Butter:**

   o In a microwave-safe bowl, melt the chopped chocolate and unsalted butter in 30-second intervals, stirring until smooth. Alternatively, melt over a double boiler.

4. **Mix Batter:**

   o Stir in the powdered sugar until well mixed.

   o Add the eggs, egg yolks, and vanilla extract. Mix until smooth.

   o Fold in the flour and a pinch of salt until just mixed.

5. **Fill Ramekins:**

   o Divide the batter evenly among the prepared ramekins.

6. **Bake the Cakes:**

   o Place the filled ramekins into the preheated air fryer oven.

   o Bake at 375°F for 10 minutes, or until the edges are set but the center is still soft.

7. **Serve:**

  o Let the cakes cool in the ramekins for 1-2 minutes.

  o Carefully run a knife around the edges of each cake to loosen it.

  o Invert the cakes onto serving plates.

Nutritional Information (per serving, based on 4 servings)

- Calories: 469

- Protein: 7g

- Total Fats: 35g

- Fiber: 2g

- Carbohydrates: 34g

Air Fried Apple Pies

Time to Prepare: 20 minutes
Cooking Time: 12 minutes
Number of Servings: 4

Ingredients

- 2 medium apples, peeled, cored, and diced

- 2 tablespoons granulated sugar

- 1/2 teaspoon of ground cinnamon

- 1/4 teaspoon of ground nutmeg

- 1 tablespoon lemon juice

- 1 tablespoon cornstarch

- 2 sheets of store-bought puff pastry, thawed

- 1 egg, beaten (for egg wash)

- 1 tablespoon coarse sugar (optional, for topping)

- Cooking spray or butter, for greasing

Instructions List

1. **Preheat the Air Fryer:**

  o Preheat the Emeril Lagasse French Door Large Air Fryer Oven to 375°F using the Air Fry function.

2. **Prepare the Apple Filling:**

  o In a bowl, combine diced apples, granulated sugar, ground cinnamon, ground nutmeg, lemon juice, and cornstarch. Mix well until apples are coated evenly.

3. **Assemble the Pies:**

  o On a lightly floured surface, roll out the puff pastry sheets. Cut each sheet into 4 squares.

  o Place a spoonful of the apple filling in the center of each pastry square.

  o Fold the pastry over the filling to form a triangle. Press the edges firmly with a fork to seal.

4. **Air Fry the Pies:**

  o Lightly grease the air fryer basket with cooking spray or butter.

  o Place the assembled pies in the air fryer basket in a single layer, leaving space between each pie.

  o Brush the tops of the pies with beaten egg and sprinkle with coarse sugar if desired.

5. **Cook the Pies:**

  o Air fry at 375°F for 12 minutes, or until the pies are golden brown and crisp.

6. **Serve:**

  o Remove the pies from the air fryer and let them cool slightly before serving.

Nutritional Information (per serving, based on 4 servings)

- Calories: 352

- Protein: 4g

- Total Fats: 21g

- Fiber: 3g

- Carbohydrates: 38g

Baked Apples with Cinnamon

Time to Prepare: 10 minutes
Cooking Time: 25 minutes
Number of Servings: 4

Ingredients

- 4 medium-sized apples (such as Gala or Honeycrisp)
- 2 tablespoons unsalted butter, melted
- 2 tablespoons brown sugar
- 1 teaspoon of ground cinnamon
- 1/4 teaspoon of ground nutmeg
- 1/4 cup of chopped walnuts or pecans (optional)
- Vanilla ice cream or whipped cream, for serving (optional)

Instructions List

1. **Preheat the Oven:**
   - Preheat the Emeril Lagasse French Door Large Air Fryer Oven to 375°F using the Bake function.

2. **Prepare the Apples:**
   - Core each apple and cut a small portion off the bottom so they can stand upright.

3. **Mix the Filling:**
   - In a small bowl, mix together melted butter, brown sugar, ground cinnamon, and ground nutmeg until well mixed.

4. **Fill the Apples:**
   - Place the cored apples upright in a baking dish or on a baking sheet lined with parchment paper.
   - Spoon the butter and sugar mixture into the center of each apple, distributing it evenly.

5. **Bake the Apples:**
   - Bake in the preheated oven at 375°F for 25 minutes, or until the apples are tender and the filling is bubbling.

6. **Serve:**
   - Remove the baked apples from the oven and let them cool slightly before serving.
   - Optionally, sprinkle chopped nuts over the top of each apple.
   - Serve warm, with vanilla ice cream or whipped cream if desired.

Nutritional Information (per serving, based on 4 servings)

- Calories: 190
- Protein: 1g
- Total Fats: 9g
- Fiber: 5g
- Carbohydrates: 31g

Air Fryer Banana Chips

Time to Prepare: 10 minutes
Cooking Time: 10-15 minutes
Number of Servings: 2-4

Ingredients

- 2 ripe bananas
- 1 tablespoon lemon juice (optional)
- Cooking spray or oil spray

Instructions List

1. **Preheat the Air Fryer Oven:**
   - Preheat the Emeril Lagasse French Door Large Air Fryer Oven to 275°F using the Air Fry function.

2. **Prepare the Bananas:**
   - Peel the bananas and slice them into thin rounds, about 1/8 inch thick.
   - If desired, toss the banana slices in lemon juice to prevent browning.

3. **Arrange in the Air Fryer:**
   - Lightly spray the air fryer basket or tray with cooking spray to prevent sticking.
   - Arrange the banana slices in a single layer in the air fryer basket or on the

tray. Avoid overcrowding to ensure even cooking.

4. **Air Fry the Banana Chips:**

   o Air fry at 275°F for 10-15 minutes, flipping the banana slices halfway through the cooking time.

   o Keep an eye on them towards the end of cooking to prevent burning, as cooking times may vary based on the thickness of the slices.

5. **Cool and Serve:**

   o Once crispy and golden brown, remove the banana chips from the air fryer and let them cool completely.

   o Serve as a healthy snack or store in an airtight container for up to a week.

Nutritional Information (per serving, based on 4 servings)

- Calories: 60
- Protein: 1g
- Total Fats: 0g
- Fiber: 2g
- Carbohydrates: 15g

Berry Crisp

Time to Prepare: 15 minutes
Cooking Time: 20-25 minutes
Number of Servings: 4-6

Ingredients

- 4 cups of mixed berries (such as strawberries, blueberries, raspberries)
- 1 tablespoon lemon juice
- 1/4 cup of granulated sugar
- 1/2 teaspoon of vanilla extract
- 1/2 cup of all-purpose flour
- 1/2 cup of old-fashioned rolled oats
- 1/4 cup of packed brown sugar
- 1/4 teaspoon of ground cinnamon
- Pinch of salt
- 1/4 cup of cold unsalted butter, diced

Instructions List

1. **Preheat the Air Fryer Oven:**

   o Preheat the Emeril Lagasse French Door Large Air Fryer Oven to 350°F using the Bake function.

2. **Prepare the Berry Filling:**

   o In a mixing bowl, combine the mixed berries, lemon juice, granulated sugar, and vanilla extract. Toss gently to coat the berries evenly.

3. **Make the Crisp Topping:**

   o In another bowl, combine the flour, oats, brown sugar, cinnamon, and salt.

   o Add the cold diced butter to the dry ingredients. Use your fingers or a pastry cutter to cut the butter into the mixture until it resembles coarse crumbs.

4. **Assemble and Bake:**

   o Transfer the berry mixture to a baking dish or an oven-safe dish that fits inside your air fryer basket or tray.

   o Sprinkle the crisp topping evenly over the berries.

5. **Air Fry the Berry Crisp:**

   o Place the baking dish with the berry crisp into the preheated air fryer oven.

   o Air fry at 350°F for 20-25 minutes, or until the topping is golden brown and the berries are bubbling.

6. **Serve Warm:**

   o Remove the berry crisp from the air fryer oven and let it cool slightly.

   o Serve warm, optionally with a scoop of vanilla ice cream or whipped cream.

Nutritional Information (per serving, based on 6 servings)

- Calories: 250
- Protein: 3g
- Total Fats: 9g
- Fiber: 5g
- Carbohydrates: 41g

Yogurt Parfaits with Air Fried Granola

Time to Prepare: 10 minutes
Cooking Time: 10 minutes
Number of Servings: 4

Ingredients

- 2 cups of old-fashioned rolled oats
- 1/2 cup of chopped nuts (such as almonds, walnuts, or pecans)
- 1/4 cup of honey or maple syrup
- 1/4 cup of coconut oil, melted
- 1 teaspoon of vanilla extract
- Pinch of salt
- 2 cups of Greek yogurt
- 1 cup of mixed berries (such as strawberries, blueberries, raspberries)
- 1/4 cup of honey or agave syrup (optional, for drizzling)

Instructions List

1. **Preheat the Air Fryer Oven:**
   - Preheat the Emeril Lagasse French Door Large Air Fryer Oven to 325°F using the Bake function.

2. **Prepare the Granola:**
   - In a mixing bowl, combine the rolled oats, chopped nuts, honey or maple syrup, melted coconut oil, vanilla extract, and a pinch of salt. Mix well until the oats are coated evenly.

3. **Air Fry the Granola:**
   - Spread the granola mixture evenly on the air fryer tray or in the air fryer basket lined with parchment paper.
   - Air fry at 325°F for 8-10 minutes, shaking or stirring halfway through, until the granola is golden brown and crisp. Keep an eye on it to prevent burning.

4. **Assemble the Parfaits:**
   - In serving glasses or bowls, layer Greek yogurt, mixed berries, and the air fried granola.

5. **Drizzle and Serve:**
   - If desired, drizzle honey or agave syrup over the yogurt parfaits for added sweetness.
   - Serve immediately and enjoy!

Nutritional Information (per serving)

- Calories: 400
- Protein: 15g
- Total Fats: 18g
- Fiber: 6g
- Carbohydrates: 45g

Air Fryer S'mores

Time to Prepare: 5 minutes
Cooking Time: 5 minutes
Number of Servings: 4

Ingredients

- 8 graham cracker squares, broken into halves
- 4 large marshmallows
- 2 oz chocolate bar, broken into squares

Instructions List

1. **Preheat the Air Fryer Oven:**
   - Preheat the Emeril Lagasse French Door Large Air Fryer Oven to 350°F using the Air Fry function.

2. **Assemble the S'mores:**

- o Place 4 graham cracker squares on a baking tray or in the air fryer basket lined with parchment paper.
- o Top each graham cracker square with a square of chocolate.

3. **Add Marshmallows:**

- o Place one large marshmallow on top of each chocolate square.

4. **Air Fry the S'mores:**

- o Place the tray or basket in the preheated air fryer oven.
- o Air fry at 350°F for about 5 minutes, or until the marshmallows are puffed and lightly browned.

5. **Serve:**

- o Remove the s'mores from the air fryer and immediately press the remaining graham cracker squares on top to create sandwiches.
- o Let cool slightly before serving.

Nutritional Information (per serving)

- Calories: 180
- Protein: 2g
- Total Fats: 7g
- Fiber: 1g
- Carbohydrates: 28g

Coconut Macaroons
Time to Prepare: 10 minutes
Cooking Time: 12 minutes
Number of Servings: 12

Ingredients

- 3 cups of shredded coconut (sweetened or unsweetened)
- 1 cup of sweetened condensed milk
- 2 teaspoons of vanilla extract
- 2 large egg whites
- Pinch of salt

Instructions List

1. **Preheat the Air Fryer Oven:**

- o Preheat the Emeril Lagasse French Door Large Air Fryer Oven to 325°F using the Bake function.

2. **Mix the Ingredients:**

- o In a large bowl, combine the shredded coconut, sweetened condensed milk, and vanilla extract. Mix well.
- o In a separate bowl, beat the egg whites with a pinch of salt until stiff peaks form.

3. **Combine the Mixtures:**

- o Gently fold the beaten egg whites into the coconut mixture until well mixed.

4. **Form Macaroons:**

- o Scoop tablespoon-sized portions of the mixture and form into compact mounds. Place them on a baking tray lined with parchment paper.

5. **Bake in the Air Fryer Oven:**

- o Place the baking tray in the preheated air fryer oven.
- o Bake at 325°F for about 12 minutes, or until the macaroons are golden brown on the outside.

6. **Cool and Serve:**

- o Remove the macaroons from the air fryer and let them cool completely on a wire rack.
- o Once cooled, store in an airtight container.

Nutritional Information (per serving)

- Calories: 220
- Protein: 3g
- Total Fats: 15g
- Fiber: 2g
- Carbohydrates: 20g

Air Fried Cheesecake Bites

Time to Prepare: 15 minutes
Cooking Time: 10 minutes
Number of Servings: 12

Ingredients

- 8 oz cream cheese, softened
- 1/4 cup of granulated sugar
- 1 teaspoon of vanilla extract
- 1 large egg
- 1/4 cup of sour cream
- 12 graham cracker squares, crushed
- 1/4 cup of melted butter
- Powdered sugar, for dusting (optional)

Instructions List

1. **Prepare the Cheesecake Mixture:**
   - In a mixing bowl, beat the softened cream cheese until smooth.
   - Add the granulated sugar and vanilla extract, and mix until well mixed.
   - Beat in the egg until fully incorporated, then mix in the sour cream until smooth.

2. **Prepare the Crust:**
   - In a separate bowl, combine the crushed graham crackers with melted butter until evenly moistened.

3. **Assemble and Form Bites:**
   - Spoon a small amount of the graham cracker mixture into the bottom of each well of a mini muffin tin, pressing down to form a crust.
   - Spoon the cheesecake mixture evenly over the crusts, filling each well almost to the top.

4. **Air Fry the Cheesecake Bites:**
   - Preheat the Emeril Lagasse French Door Large Air Fryer Oven to 325°F using the Bake function.
   - Place the filled mini muffin tin into the preheated air fryer oven.
   - Air fry at 325°F for about 10 minutes, or until the cheesecake bites are set and lightly golden on top.

5. **Cool and Serve:**
   - Remove the cheesecake bites from the air fryer oven and let them cool in the muffin tin for a few minutes.
   - Carefully remove the cheesecake bites from the muffin tin and transfer them to a wire rack to cool completely.
   - Dust with powdered sugar before serving, if desired.

Nutritional Information (per serving)

- Calories: 160
- Protein: 3g
- Total Fats: 12g
- Fiber: 0.5g
- Carbohydrates: 11g

Peanut Butter Cookies

Time to Prepare: 15 minutes
Cooking Time: 10 minutes
Number of Servings: 12 cookies

Ingredients

- 1 cup of creamy peanut butter
- 1/2 cup of granulated sugar
- 1/2 cup of brown sugar
- 1 large egg
- 1 teaspoon of vanilla extract
- 1/2 teaspoon of baking soda
- Pinch of salt

Instructions List

1. **Prepare the Cookie Dough:**
   - In a mixing bowl, combine the creamy peanut butter, granulated

sugar, and brown sugar. Mix until well mixed and creamy.

o Add the egg, vanilla extract, baking soda, and pinch of salt. Mix until all ingredients are thoroughly incorporated and the dough is smooth.

2. **Shape and Chill the Dough:**

o Scoop out portions of the dough and roll them into balls, about 1 tablespoon each.

o Place the cookie dough balls on a baking sheet lined with parchment paper or silicone mat. Use a fork to create a crisscross pattern on top of each cookie, gently pressing down to flatten them slightly.

3. **Chill the Cookies:**

o Place the baking sheet with the shaped cookies in the refrigerator for at least 30 minutes to chill. This helps the cookies maintain their shape while baking.

4. **Preheat and Air Fry:**

o Preheat the Emeril Lagasse French Door Large Air Fryer Oven to 350°F using the Bake function.

5. **Bake the Cookies:**

o Place the chilled cookie dough balls into the preheated air fryer oven basket or on the air fryer trays, ensuring they are spaced apart to allow for even cooking.

o Air fry at 350°F for about 10 minutes, or until the cookies are golden brown and set.

6. **Cool and Serve:**

o Remove the cookies from the air fryer oven and let them cool on the baking sheet for a few minutes.

o Transfer the cookies to a wire rack to cool completely before serving.

Nutritional Information (per cookie)

- Calories: 210

- Protein: 6g

- Total Fats: 13g

- Fiber: 2g

- Carbohydrates: 19g

Air Fryer Brownies

Time to Prepare: 15 minutes
Cooking Time: 20 minutes
Number of Servings: 9 brownies

Ingredients

- 1/2 cup of unsalted butter

- 1 cup of granulated sugar

- 2 large eggs

- 1 teaspoon of vanilla extract

- 1/3 cup unsweetened cocoa powder

- 1/2 cup of all-purpose flour

- 1/4 teaspoon of salt

- 1/4 teaspoon of baking powder

Instructions List

1. **Prepare the Brownie Batter:**

o In a microwave-safe bowl, melt the unsalted butter in the microwave until completely melted.

o Add the granulated sugar to the melted butter and mix until well mixed.

o Stir in the eggs and vanilla extract until smooth.

2. **Mix Dry Ingredients:**

o In a separate bowl, sift together the unsweetened cocoa powder, all-purpose flour, salt, and baking powder.

o Gradually add the dry ingredients to the wet ingredients, mixing until just mixed. Do not overmix.

3. **Preheat and Prepare Air Fryer:**

o Preheat your Emeril Lagasse French Door Large Air Fryer Oven to 325°F using the Bake function.

4. **Prepare the Pan:**

   o Line an 8x8-inch baking pan with parchment paper or lightly grease it with butter.

5. **Bake the Brownies:**

   o Pour the brownie batter into the prepared baking pan, spreading it evenly with a spatula.

6. **Air Fry the Brownies:**

   o Place the baking pan with the brownie batter into the preheated air fryer oven.

   o Air fry at 325°F for about 20 minutes, or until a toothpick inserted into the center comes out with a few moist crumbs.

7. **Cool and Serve:**

   o Remove the brownies from the air fryer oven and let them cool completely in the pan on a wire rack.

   o Once cooled, lift the brownies out of the pan using the parchment paper and cut into 9 squares.

Nutritional Information (per brownie)

- Calories: 240
- Protein: 3g
- Total Fats: 12g
- Fiber: 2g
- Carbohydrates: 32g

Spiced Pumpkin Seeds

Time to Prepare: 10 minutes
Cooking Time: 15 minutes
Number of Servings: 4 servings

Ingredients

- 1 cup of raw pumpkin seeds (pepitas), cleaned and dried
- 1 tablespoon olive oil
- 1/2 teaspoon of ground cinnamon
- 1/4 teaspoon of ground nutmeg
- 1/4 teaspoon of ground ginger
- 1/4 teaspoon of ground cloves
- 1/4 teaspoon of salt
- 1 tablespoon granulated sugar (optional, for a sweeter flavor)

Instructions List

1. **Prepare Pumpkin Seeds:**

   o Preheat your Emeril Lagasse French Door Large Air Fryer Oven to 325°F using the Bake function.

   o In a bowl, toss the cleaned and dried pumpkin seeds with olive oil until evenly coated.

2. **Season Pumpkin Seeds:**

   o Add ground cinnamon, ground nutmeg, ground ginger, ground cloves, salt, and granulated sugar (if using) to the bowl with the pumpkin seeds. Mix well to evenly distribute the spices.

3. **Air Fry the Pumpkin Seeds:**

   o Spread the seasoned pumpkin seeds in a single layer on the air fryer basket or tray.

4. **Cook in Air Fryer:**

   o Place the basket or tray into the preheated air fryer oven.

   o Air fry at 325°F for about 15 minutes, shaking or stirring halfway through cooking, until the pumpkin seeds are golden brown and crispy.

5. **Cool and Serve:**

   o Remove the pumpkin seeds from the air fryer and let them cool completely before serving.

Nutritional Information (per serving)

- Calories: 180
- Protein: 8g

- Total Fats: 15g
- Fiber: 2g
- Carbohydrates: 4g

Air Fried Pecan Pie Bites
Time to Prepare: 15 minutes
Cooking Time: 12 minutes
Number of Servings: 8 bites

Ingredients

- 1 sheet of puff pastry, thawed
- 1/2 cup of pecans, chopped
- 1/4 cup of brown sugar
- 2 tablespoons maple syrup
- 1 tablespoon unsalted butter, melted
- 1/2 teaspoon of vanilla extract
- 1/4 teaspoon of salt
- 1 egg, beaten (for egg wash)
- Powdered sugar, for dusting (optional)

Instructions List

1. **Prepare the Filling:**
   - In a bowl, mix together chopped pecans, brown sugar, maple syrup, melted butter, vanilla extract, and salt until well mixed.

2. **Prepare the Puff Pastry:**
   - Roll out the thawed puff pastry sheet on a lightly floured surface. Cut into 8 squares.

3. **Assemble the Pecan Pie Bites:**
   - Place a spoonful of the pecan filling onto the center of each puff pastry square.
   - Fold the corners of each square towards the center, pinching the edges to seal and form a small packet.

4. **Preheat the Air Fryer Oven:**
   - Preheat your Emeril Lagasse French Door Large Air Fryer Oven to 350°F using the Air Fry function.

5. **Air Fry the Pecan Pie Bites:**
   - Brush the tops of the pecan pie bites with beaten egg (egg wash).
   - Place the bites in a single layer on the air fryer basket or tray.
   - Air fry at 350°F for about 12 minutes, or until the pastry is golden brown and crispy.

6. **Cool and Serve:**
   - Remove the pecan pie bites from the air fryer and let them cool slightly.
   - Optionally, dust with powdered sugar before serving.

Nutritional Information (per serving, 1 bite)

- Calories: 248
- Protein: 3g
- Total Fats: 16g
- Fiber: 1g
- Carbohydrates: 25g

MEASUREMENT CONVERSION TABLE

Measurement	Imperial (US)	Metric
Volume		
1 teaspoon of	1 teaspoon	5 milliliters
1 tablespoon	1 tablespoon	15 milliliters
1 fluid ounce	1 fl oz	30 milliliters
1 cup	1 cup	240 milliliters
1 pint	1 pt	473 milliliters
1 quart	1 qt	0.95 liters
1 gallon	1 gal	3.8 liters
Weight		
1 ounce	1 oz	28 grams
1 pound	1 lb	454 grams
Temperature		
32°F	32°F	0°C
212°F	212°F	100°C
Other		
1 stick of butter	1 stick	113 grams

CONCLUSION

RECIPES INDEX

Grilled Portobello Mushrooms 71

Hawaiian Pizza 44

Herb-Crusted Chicken Cutlets 27

Herb-Roasted Potatoes 61

Honey Garlic Chicken Wings 20

Honey Glazed Carrots 62

Honey Mustard Pork Tenderloin 32

Honey Soy Glazed Cod 51

Korean BBQ Beef Short Ribs 34

Lemon Herb Roasted Chicken 19

Lemon Herb Salmon 48

Maple Bacon Donuts 10

Maple Glazed Pork Chops 31

Margherita Pizza 38

Meatball Subs 42

Mediterranean Veggie Wrap 46

Mini Quiches 12

Mozzarella-Stuffed Meatballs 17

Parmesan Crusted Tilapia 52

Peanut Butter Cookies 83

Pepperoni Calzones 42

Philly Cheesesteak Sandwich 39

Pulled Pork Sandwich 45

Quinoa and Veggie Bowls 66

Roasted Beet Salad 64

Roasted Cauliflower 59

Roasted Garlic Brussels Sprouts 73

Shrimp Scampi 53

Spiced Pumpkin Seeds 85

Spicy Buffalo Chicken Pizza 46

Spicy Italian Sausage Links 36

Spicy Sriracha Chicken Nuggets 27

Spicy Tuna Steaks 56

Spinach and Feta Stuffed Croissants 15

Stuffed Bell Peppers 60

Stuffed Chicken Breasts with Spinach and Cheese 24

Stuffed Mushrooms 12

Stuffed Pork Loin with Apple and Sage 33

Sweet Potato and Black Bean Tacos 69

Sweet Potato Fries 59

Sweet Potato Hash Browns 16

Teriyaki Chicken Skewers 26

Teriyaki Glazed Pork Belly 37

Teriyaki Salmon Bites 54

Turkey Club Sandwich 43

Vegan Eggplant Fries 72

Vegan Stuffed Mushrooms 74

Vegan Stuffed Peppers 68

Vegetable Frittata 11

Veggie Supreme Pizza 40

Yogurt Parfaits with Air Fried Granola 81

Made in the USA
Monee, IL
02 December 2024

72032787R00052